Muddling Along or Unity:

Confessions of a Recovering Jerk

David L. Freeman

Printed in the United States of America
First Printing, 2019

Publisher: Dialog and Resolve LLC
Springfield, Missouri
www.dialogandresolve.com

Scripture quotations are taken from the Holy Bible, New American Standard, copyright ©1960, 1692, 1968, 1971, 1972, 1973, 1975, 1995 by The Lockman Foundation. Used by permission of The Zondervan Corporation, Grand Rapids, Michigan 49530. All rights reserved.

Dedication:

To Jesus, my family, the staff and participants at Discovery Ministries, and the Church:

Thank you for graciously bearing the brunt of my learning curve.

Thank you:

In early 2017, during my first mentor meeting with my friend, Jason, he said, "There is really no reason for us to talk about anything else until you finish the book." He then told me how to gather a team around me to get it done, and how to self-publish. Thanks for the kick-start!

To my reading and editing team, thank you for the accountability and great insights along the way: Amanda, Becky, Brenyn, Colette, Gary, Jason, Jeff, Jeremy, Jill, Katherine, Kiersten, LaVonna, Linda, and Ric.

Contents

Definitions

Team – n. Two or more people joining efforts.

    ex. Marriage, family, church, business, non-profit, government

Disagreement – n. a key component of effective team performance.

    ex. "I see things from a much different perspective than you."

Conflict – n. a key component of team destruction.

    ex. "I see things from a much different perspective than you *and* you are a jerk! Why do you insist on existing in my presence?! The world would have been better off today if you had stayed in bed!"

Adrenaline – n. the chemical responsible for the fight or flight responses that turn a disagreement into a conflict.

Unity – n. when a team functions at 55-60% of theoretical team potential – a.k.a. performing.

80% are Stuck

In 2005, the tension and conflict mounted in our office, so that by the end of the year, I submitted an evaluation basically saying, "I think I need to leave because I am causing so much conflict." I shared a co-directorship with Gary at Discovery Ministries, a wilderness adventure ministry dedicated to teaching Christians personal responsibility and teamwork. We both had extensive Bible training, strong private devotional lives, and strong families. We had honed our facilitation skills during years of teaching people to live like Jesus. We each fulfilled our individual responsibilities and roles effectively; however, we hadn't been able to mesh our personalities and approaches to ministry to become a cohesive team.

The challenge overwhelmed me. I felt guilty because I figured if anybody should know how to get along and work effectively together, we should. I became discouraged.

Then Jesus did His thing!

That fall some last-minute doors opened, allowing me to begin a master's degree. I laughed wryly when I realized the only class option remaining was Interpersonal Conflict Resolution. But within a couple of weeks, I learned a statistic that changed my outlook for the Discovery Ministries team and set the foundation of grace on which we started to rebuild. According to Dr. Susan Wheelan[1], an Organization Development professor and consultant, over 80% of teams get stuck in early stages of team development. Wheelan describes four team stages, which correspond to Dr. Bruce Tuckman's well-known "forming-storming-norming-performing" model.[2] Tuckman was a pioneering group dynamics researcher. "Forming" is when the team first comes together and just does what the leader says because members are too uncomfortable to voice opinions. "Storming" is when members become comfortable enough in the group to begin voicing their opinions, which cause conflict. This is where 80% of groups get stuck. They cycle from "storming," to having conflicts instead of disagreements, then revert to "forming" because "storming" is too uncomfortable and challenging. If groups develop skills to work through disagreements they progress to "norming," where they learn to use their different perspectives and opinions to create plans and systems to meet group goals. Groups then progress to "performing," what the Bible calls "unity," when they are consistently making effective progress toward meeting their goals. A key indicator of a "performing" team is many disagreements, which are quickly resolved.

In this book, I am going to simplify the team stages into two: "muddling along," where 80% of groups are stuck, and "unity."

I jumped on the 80% statistic because it rang true with the staff's observations and experiences, working with thousands of teams. I realized our situation was not abnormal, but rather we were stuck in this crazy world where even mature Christians struggle with the challenge of "unity."

I am convinced the 80% statistic applies to churches, families, non-profits, businesses, government agencies, sports teams . . . I think you get the picture.

Another 80% statistic pointed out at a conference is that 80% of non-profits go out of existence within five years of the founder leaving the organization. Hmmm, could there be a correlation between the two statistics? It makes sense that an organization lacking the skill to work through disagreements would not be able to complete the massive challenge of the first leadership transition.

Gary had founded Discovery Ministries and was planning to retire within a few years. We realized that if the camp was to thrive under new leadership, we had a lot of work to do, and Jesus provided the tools just in time.

Once we acquired good conflict resolution models, we quickly formulated a plan. Gary, Becky (Gary's wife), Colette (my wife), and I met most weeks for two hours to talk about everything we had not talked about since Colette and I joined the ministry ten years earlier. Our meetings began with the question, "What aggravation has popped up in your mind as you have mulled over what we talked about in previous meetings?" We were determined to meet until there were no more unresolved aggravations. It took six months.

At the end of summer 2006, my evaluation read drastically different from my evaluation six months earlier, "This is the first time I have ended a summer feeling refreshed, rather than feeling like I need to go away for several weeks to recuperate. Unity is wonderful!"

Jesus worked that miracle just in time. At the end of 2006, two couples who had completed internships made a proposal to join with Discovery Ministries and launch a new outreach. I readily agreed to their proposal because I felt we had learned how to create and maintain effective unity and could mentor the new staff. From that point forward, the staff continually trained in and lived many of the skills in this book.

February 2012, Gary and I stepped down from co-directorship at Discovery Ministries and handed the reins over to the couples who had joined us in 2006. I am writing this sentence in November of 2018, and Discovery

Ministries is thriving. It is possible to overcome the 80% statistics!

There were also wonderful personal side effects of the skills we developed as a staff at Discovery Ministries. For instance, I became a better church member. Around 2007, a member of my church came to me and said, "I don't know what you do, but when you are here our meetings are cordial and productive; when you are not, we bicker and don't get much done." When I heard those words, I celebrated Jesus' work in my life; however, that moment was not the biggest indicator of the change in my life. The biggest indicators were at home.

My prayer is you enjoy reading these pages as you find solutions for the 80% groups in which you exist. Come on! Join me as we use adrenaline sports training principles to master these Biblical skills, so we live in "unity" at home, work, and church.

Part I—The Challenges

Beloved, do not be surprised at the fiery

ordeal among you. . . . – 1 Peter 4:12

It was the biggest gut-wrenching challenge most of us had ever faced.

Sunday, May 22, 2011, from 5:41 p.m. to 6:01 p.m. the deadliest tornado in the Midwest since 1947 wiped out one third of Joplin, Missouri. It resembled a bomb-blast site one mile wide and six miles long through the middle of town. Monday, May 23, part of the Discovery Ministries staff went to Joplin to help. We ended up designing and starting up the city's main receiving and distribution center located at College Heights Christian Church.

When we arrived, there was no plan in place to operate a point of distribution at the church, and we had zero experience with disaster response distribution. The gymnasium bleachers were already filled from seat to ceiling with trash bags of donated clothes, two semi-trucks full of water were parked outside the city waiting to unload at the church the next morning, and we were leading a volunteer team of people who had instantly lost much of life as they knew it, including family and friends.

On Tuesday afternoon, May 24, Jay St Clair, the church's Community Outreach Pastor, said, "I think we are operating

7

at about 60% capacity and that is about as good as we can do." When I heard Jay say that, I was thrilled and deeply satisfied; because a few months earlier, while writing the first draft for this book, I concluded that 60% of possible teamwork capacity is about as good as any group can hope to achieve.

Think about it. If 100% is every person in the group:

1. Having the correct gifting/training for their position.
2. Having expert skill in interpersonal communication, creative thinking, decision making, and effective meetings.
3. Showing up 100% healthy and focused physically, mentally, emotionally, and spiritually every moment of every day.

then 60% seems accurate.

Yes, I am positing that a group achieves unity when operating at 55-60% of possible teamwork capacity. One side effect of this 60% definition is you can give yourself and others grace when you and your group do not perform perfectly. Many individuals and groups could benefit from giving up the frustration and tension that comes with the dream of perfection.

Is shooting for 60% good enough?

On Wednesday, two days after the tornado, Randy Gariss, the lead pastor, received a phone call, "I apologize for interrupting. I know you are busy, but I want to tell you that I am with FEMA and just walked through your facility. I was inspired. I have been involved with disaster response for over 15 years, and I have never seen any organization functioning that efficiently, that quickly after a disaster." By Wednesday evening we had distributed food, clothing, and other essentials to over 2,000 people, fed over 2,000 meals to volunteers and victims, and had unbelievable opportunities for ministry, including one request for baptism. Yes, 60% is an effective target.

How does a group move from "muddling along" to being in "unity?" The first step in creating an effective solution is to understand the extent of the obstacle. "Unity" is more challenging than herding cats.

Chapter 1—Unity Requires Common Goals and Plans

Make my joy complete by being of the same mind, maintaining the same love, united in spirit, intent on one purpose

– Philippians 2:2

My wife and I really enjoy tandem canoeing, and we can make a canoe dance, even in raging whitewater. However, we did have to learn to laugh, rather than get frustrated, about two realities. Most of our paddling challenges went away after I took paddling classes and communication training, but two seem permanent due to our vastly different personalities and perspectives of the world.

Yes, you read correctly, it is hard to admit, but I was the one who needed training. You see, in our early paddling years we earned the nickname "the dear-jerk duo" because we provided a lot of entertainment by our sloppy whitewater paddling. I had the unfortunate habit of frequently yelling, "Paddle dear!" Then, one time, while we were sitting with a bunch of other paddlers in calm water, I asked, "Hey, Colette, are you hot?" When she said, "yes," I tipped over our canoe. She came out of the cold water, laughing, hitting my helmeted-head with her paddle, and yelling, "Jerk, jerk, jerk!" The consensus in our paddling group was I deserved everything I got. Soon after that head-whacking event, we began having children, which took Colette out of the paddling scene for about seven years. During that time, I took several paddling classes and trained diligently, so I could become a competent paddling instructor. When Colette stepped back into a tandem canoe with me seven years later, we made the canoe dance. Obviously, it was not my wife who needed to improve. It is the story of our life in so many areas. I must work and train for years to catch up with Colette's natural ability.

I digress. We still have two paddling challenges.

First, if one of us says, "Let's get behind that rock," often, we are looking at different rocks. What happens when we are in the same canoe trying to get behind different rocks? We work harder than we need to, have zero control, look like panicked raw-beginners, and provide entertainment for spectators.

Second, even if we are looking at the same rock, my wife and I pick different routes to the rock. There are multiple ways to get to any spot in a river:

1. Ferry—go straight across current—with the canoe facing upstream or downstream.
2. Surf—ride waves with little effort—with the canoe facing upstream or downstream.
3. Jump in and swim.

These are only a few of the options. What happens when we are in the same canoe trying to get behind the same rock using different plans? Again, we work harder than we need to, have zero control, look like panicked raw-beginners, and provide entertainment for spectators.

Sound familiar? How many times have you been in a meeting where the meeting gets really challenging because one person wants to figure out what we are doing for tomorrow's party, and another person wants to decide about purchasing a major asset. In other words, they have different goals in the same meeting.

How about the family vacation challenge? One or more people want to sleep late, lie on the beach, read, do nothing for the rest of the day, then repeat that schedule the next day. Another one or more want to get up early, see and do all there is within a hundred-mile radius of the beach, go to bed late, then repeat that schedule the next day. The family members have different plans for the same beach-vacation goal.

One determinant I use to see if a group is functioning in "unity" is to (if possible):

1. Stop all activity.
2. Gather the group.

3. Give each person a piece of paper and have them write what goal(s) we are currently pursuing and what plan(s) we are using to pursue the goal(s).

4. Then compare all the answers.

Ideally, each piece of paper would have the same basic answers. Sadly, all I usually have time to do is have the group, in unison, repeat the three or four main goals and plans; however, if the goal(s) and plan(s) are vital, I will circle up the team, and go around the circle one at a time having each person say the goal(s) and plan(s).

This concept is nothing new. Many groups have many meetings trying to craft vision statements, mission statements, themes or whatever else the latest books call macro- and micro-level goals and plans.

What Colette and I have learned paddling, and every other challenge we tackle together in life, is we must not leave the calm water until we have an effective meeting to ensure we are aiming for the same next calm water and have the same plan in mind to get there. The more challenging the goal and plan, the more deliberate and lengthier the meeting. If we start to flounder in wild water, we immediately do whatever it takes to get to calm water, so we can re-group, i.e. have an effective meeting to ensure a common goal and plan.

It takes both skill and effort from every team member to get, and maintain, common goals and plans. Most groups lack the skill, and do not want to take the time or do the hard work of staying together. It is easier to complain, gossip, and keep moving.

Why is it sooooo hard to create and sustain common goals and plans?

Chapter 2—*TRIPS*, the Five Levels of Goals

For they all seek after their own interests . . . – Philippians 2:21

Get ready to have your over-simplified summaries of arguments blown away. Are you sitting down?

There are five levels of goals during most interactions between people. I learned the first four levels from Dr. William Wilmot and Dr. Joyce Hocker[3], both are conflict resolution professors and practitioners. Dr. Peter Senge[4], an Organization Development guru, introduced me to the last level, a systems perspective. To remember them I use the acronym *TRIPS* and the image of an iceberg.

One reason I like the *TRIPS* acronym is when you take trips with other people they can be negative or positive experiences depending on what happens and people's reactions. There is no such thing as bad weather; just inadequate clothes, training, and attitudes. Disagreements are much the same as trips in this sense.

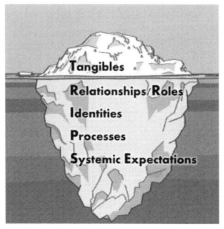

As for the iceberg, notice the tangible goals (T) are on the small surface above the water and the rest of the goals (**RIPS**) are underneath.

Actually, **TRIPS** icebergs look more like real icebergs. Real icebergs often have multiple peaks (T) above the water that rise off the same huge hidden berg (**RIPS**) under the water. Here is a more accurate picture of (T) (*RIPS*).

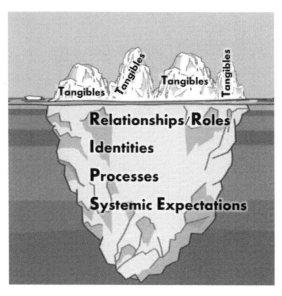

TRIPS illustrates why Colette and I disagree about when to eat lunch today, when one of us suddenly says, "You did this same thing to me last year when we were trying to decide what car to buy." There is some unmet (**RIPS**) goal in today's lunch decision that was also unmet in last year's car decision.

Let's learn more about the five levels of goals

(*T*) Tangibles

Tangible (*T*) goals are the easiest to understand and discuss. They are what we can explain and measure using our five senses—touch, taste, see, smell, hear. While Colette and I are paddling together as instructors in a whitewater training class, some of the tangible goals are:

1. Which rock do we get behind next?
2. When do we eat snacks and lunch?
3. Is that a venomous or non-venomous snake about to drop off the limb into our boat?
4. What is the best answer for the technique question that participant asked?
5. Is it time to stop the event because of risky weather or do we keep going?

These are the tangible goals on the surface of our disagreements. Since they are easiest to recognize, they are the most discussed goals during disagreements; however, they are the *least* important goals on which to agree for satisfying resolution.

The Underlying (*RIPS*)

To live in "unity," the most important goals to resolve are the (*RIPS*). Imagine with me, if you will, that each of us has a recipe box stored in the recesses of our brains. The box has four sections—*R, I, P,* and *S*. Each section is full of cards. Each card records a goal.

The *big* challenge is most of those cards are written in invisible ink that only our adrenaline can read. In many instances, we are working hard to achieve goals we don't even realize we have. If they remain unrealized and unevaluated, they often trigger the adrenaline that pushes disagreements into conflicts.

Let's find out what is written on those cards.

(*R*) Relationships/Roles

In some settings the word "relationships" is awkward, or makes people uneasy. It is wise to use the word "roles" in those settings.

The (*R)* sections of each of our recipe boxes are full of cards for all the roles in life. When we encounter a person in a role, we pull out our card for that role to figure out how we expect that person to behave. When we find ourselves in a role, we pull out our card for that role to figure out how we expect ourselves to behave. The challenge is many of us have different things written on our cards for the same role.

For instance, let's pretend I am the paddling instructor and you are one of the students. As each of us arrives for the training session, somewhere deep inside our mental wanderings we pull out our "Paddling Instructor" card that shows what each of us think are the roles of the paddling instructor. If they look like the following, we are probably in for a challenging interpersonal day.

Mine:

Paddling Instructor

1. Tells students how to move gear to the river.
2. Tells students which boat and paddles to use.
3. Should decide when to eat.
4. Plays hard on whitewater to model what is possible.

Yours:

Paddling Instructor

1. Should move students' gear to the river.
2. Should let students pick boat and paddles.
3. Should let me decide when to eat.
4. Watches me all day to see how I'm doing.

19

Remember, our relationships/roles cards are goals for us. Most of us, on a subconscious level, want to make sure the people around us are functioning according to what we have written on our card, even if we don't realize what is written on the card.

Think for a moment about all the different relationships/roles there are in life:

1. Husband and Wife.
2. Parent and Child.
3. Sibling and Sibling.
4. Owner and Manager.
5. Manager and Employee.
6. Co-worker and Co-worker.
7. Doctor and Patient.
8. Nurse and Patient.
9. Pastor and Church Member.
10. Pastor and Staff Member.
11. Police officer and Citizen.
12. Etc.

All day long each of us are interacting with people who have different instructions on their cards than we have on our cards.

(*I*) Identity

The second section of cards each of us carries in our life recipes box is our (*I*)dentity cards. Identity is who I tell myself I am. We each have multiple cards. Remember, most of us do not know, at a conscious level, what is written on most of these cards. We naturally write about 3- to 6-word summaries on each card. Those words begin with "I am" or "I am not." Here are some common ones.

1. I am smart.
2. I am not smart.
3. I am right.
4. I am wrong.
5. I am worthy of respect.
6. I am not worthy of respect.
7. I am worthy of love.
8. I am not worthy of love.
9. I am good at . . . .
10. I am not good at . . . .
11. I am a good Christian.
12. Etc.

These identity cards are goals for us. We want people to treat us as if they agree with these cards, and if we perceive they don't agree with our card(s), our adrenaline quickly goes to work.

For instance, if I have an identity card that reads "I am a good father" and my wife gives me an exasperated look because I left a child behind at the last rest stop, I will probably have the sudden urge to defend myself. Unfortunately, in the early days of our marriage, I most often defended myself by going on the attack and pointing out what my wife had done wrong in the past. That dysfunction contained very little fun.

(*P*) Process

The third section of cards is the (*P*)rocess cards. These are the cards that each of us has for how to resolve disagreements. Conflict resolution professors Thomas and Kilmann[5] showed that even though we may have several cards, one for each situation, all the cards state one of five basic conflict resolution strategies (see Chapter 13 for details about each strategy). Each strategy has pros and cons. Without training, we tend to choose the same style for all situations. Like a carpenter who only uses a hammer, it works well when the situation is appropriate; not so well the other times. Each of us tries to get those around us to resolve disagreements using our own preferred style. To make it worse, the styles often aggravate each other rather than bring resolution.

For instance, if you and I are co-workers standing at the water cooler having a conversation that suddenly turns into a disagreement, we each "pull out cards." What if they looked like this?

Mine:

> ### Resolve public disagreements at work by competing:
>
> 1. Get louder.
> 2. Give increasingly persuasive arguments.
> 3. If the co-worker walks away, follow until he/she admits I am right.

Yours:

> ### Resolve public disagreements at work by avoiding:
>
> 1. Get quiet.
> 2. Make a quick excuse and leave.
> 3. Get to my office and close and lock the door.

Do you see how our (**P**)rocess cards could easily lead to an interesting scene, for everyone else, of me pounding on your door yelling several convincing arguments? Not good.

(**S**) Systemic Expectations

The fourth section of recipe cards is (**S**)ystemic Expectations. Each of us belong to many groups, and each of those groups has (un)written and (un)spoken rules, roles, and relationships to which it expects each member to conform. Those expectations are goals I bring into every decision, even decisions made outside of that particular group. For instance, when I am a paddling instructor with Discovery Ministries, I cannot just make decisions as David Freeman. I must also consider the following groups:

1. Discovery Ministries Instructors.
2. MO Dept. of Conservation Land Users.
3. Dept. of Natural Resources Land Users.
4. Wilderness Medical Associates' Wilderness First Responders.
5. American Canoe Association Instructors.
6. Family Members.
7. Local Church Members.
8. Jesus Followers of the Universal Church.

A classic example of (*S*)ystemic Expectations is the Woody Allen skit where a couple are sitting talking on their bed. Soon the wife's mother is sitting on the bed talking into the wife's ear, then the wife says those exact words to her husband. Next you see the husband's mother on the bed talking into his ear, then he says those exact words to his wife. Before long the bed is full of people telling the husband and wife what to say to each other. I think you get the point.

Another type of (**S**)ystemic Expectations is the written rules and regulations a group puts in place. This is where Senge's studies shed great light on conflicts. In *The Fifth Discipline*[4] he does an excellent job proving that often an individual gets in trouble when the true culprit is the dysfunctional system of rules we have created. This happens in work, church, and home. One example—I berated one of my children for not doing the laundry, and later realized she was the victim of a flawed system I had set in place (more on that story in Chapter 11 - Forgiveness).

Each of us carries (**S**)ystemic Expectations cards that contain goals we feel pressured to meet, and we bring those goals into our disagreements.

We discuss **TRIPS** goals several times throughout this book. For now, understand that:

1. They exist.
2. Not every conversation contains all the **TRIPS** goals.
3. They are present in different combinations in most conversations.
4. Many of them exist at a subconscious level, which causes challenge in every disagreement, because thwarted subconscious goals trigger adrenaline.

Thus, interpersonal conflict resolution is like an adrenaline sport.

Chapter 3—Adrenaline

He who is slow to anger is better than the mighty, And he who rules his spirit, than he who captures a city. – Proverbs 16:32

Usually, if someone gets upset during a disagreement, that person has some (**RIPS**) goals that are being thwarted. When we perceive, at a subconscious level, that a (**RIPS**) goal is being thwarted, our body dumps adrenaline into our system just as it would if our physical body was being attacked. Adrenaline and thwarted (**RIPS**) goals are like a match and kerosene that turns disagreements into conflict conflagrations.

As a rule, adrenaline causes us to act in one of four ways: fight, flight, freeze, or faint. However, there is a fifth option—flow. Flow is when your skills and training are adequate for the challenge, so you perform well with or without adrenaline. The following chart illustrates when adrenaline kicks in turning a disagreement (flow) into a conflict (fight, flight, freeze, or faint). Notice that whether a goal is conscious or subconscious—has visible ink or invisible ink on the card—the moment we perceive our goal is thwarted the adrenaline responses begin. If the goal is known, I have the option of Flow even if it is thwarted.

	I perceive goal is achievable	I perceive goal is thwarted
Goal I know I have	Flow	Perhaps Flow Fight Flight Freeze Faint
Goal I do not realize I have (Subconscious)	Flow	Fight Flight Freeze Faint

Most people have little understanding and training in disagreeing skillfully. Which means they quickly move into conflict (adrenaline reactions) soon after a disagreement begins.

Let's review what we have learned so far in The Challenges chapters:

1. Unity requires common goals and plans.
2. There are five levels of goals.
3. Many goals are at a subconscious level.
4. Adrenaline kicks in when we perceive goals are thwarted.

But, wait! There is more that makes unity like herding cats.

Chapter 4—Goals are Constantly Changing

There is a time for every event under heaven

– Ecclesiastes 3:1

If you are blessed enough to be in climate-controlled buildings, you probably have first-hand experience with the thermostat tango: one person walks by the thermostat to turn it up; a few minutes later another person walks by to turn it down. Each person is doing the most natural thing in the world, trying to adjust circumstances to maintain homeostasis, which is personal comfort. The challenge comes when one person's adjustment inadvertently pulls another person out of homeostasis. This happens all day long in many ways.

Dialectical Tensions is a theory that most accurately describes what happens to goals. Also, I like the theory because I like saying the words "dialectical tensions." Go ahead. Try it. Say "dialectical tensions" five times.

The theory goes something like this: most of us have pairs of goals in life that seem to be mutually exclusive, and yet, they are both truths that help us achieve homeostasis and satisfaction in life.

For instance, I want to be warm and I want to be cool. Really, what I want is to be comfortable. The moment I realize I am too warm, I have the goal of getting cooler. The moment I realize I am too cool, I have the goal of getting warmer. I go through any day making frequent adjustments trying to get warmer and cooler. I adjust the thermostat on the car air conditioning, roll windows up and down, put on a coat, take off a coat, switch the coat for a lighter or thicker coat, move to the sunshine, move to the shade, put on a hat, take off a hat, move a hat further up my head or lower over my ears, adjust the thermostat . . . I think you get the point.

Picture with me, if you will, a tug-of-war match between Warm and Cool. You are sitting in a lawn chair between Warm and Cool. Warm has a rope tied to your chair on one side and Cool has a rope tied to your chair on the other side. Your goal is for your chair to remain still so you can relax— homeostasis. When you feel a tug from either side, you have a little aggravation. When the tug gets aggravating enough, you do something to give the opposite side more strength. Your chair scoots across the ground in both directions many times a day.

To make the picture more accurate, picture yourself sitting in a lawn chair precariously suspended in the middle of a sphere held in place by many opposing goals. Too hard of a tug on any one rope can cause one or more ropes on the other side of the sphere to need adjusting to keep you comfortable in your chair. Relaxing in your chair is homeostasis. If many opposing tugging ropes are precariously suspending you in mid-air, how often do you think you will be sitting in the lawn chair kicked back with your hands behind your head resting comfortably in homeostasis? Hardly at all! You will be frantically tending all the ropes to keep your chair from tipping.

This is a picture of what is happening internally and externally with each of us. No wonder Philo of Alexandria said, "Be kind, for everyone you meet is fighting a great battle."

Here are a few dialectical tension goals:

1. I/We need to be content with 60% of perfection, and striving for perfection makes me/us better.
2. I want to be needed, and I need my space.
3. I need to be heard, and I need to listen.
4. I/We need to be serious, and we need to have fun.
5. I must go to the bathroom, and I can wait a long time.
6. I/We need to live peacefully, and I/we need to function with a sense of urgency.
7. I/We need to build relationships, and I/We do not have enough time to maintain all relationships.
8. I/We need to get disagreements out in the open, and I/we need to avoid conflict.
9. I/We want to have influence, and it is nice to sit back and let others make decisions.

10. I am right, and I need to consider others' perspectives.
11. The early bird gets the worm, and haste makes waste.
12. We are designed to experience Jesus corporately, and He speaks to us individually.

The theory of dialectical tensions suggests that we all go through every day constantly adjusting our conscious and sub-conscious goals and plans. Have you ever had a meeting, worked long and hard to hammer out goals and plans, left the meeting thinking we are moving in a good direction, then have someone from that meeting call the next day wanting to make changes to the goals and plans? Dialectical tensions strike again. As one minister told me, "We just try to keep the 'fun' in 'dysfunctional.'"

But wait! There is one more element of dialectical tensions to conceptualize.

Chapter 5—There are a Mind-Boggling Number of Groups in Any Group

So we, who are many, are one body in Christ – Romans 12:5

You are standing in a room alone. Metaphorically, you are sitting in your lawn chair, trying to maintain homeostasis, suspended in mid-air by many ropes. I walk into the room. All of us, metaphorically speaking, are sitting in our lawn chairs precariously suspended in mid-air by a sphere of many opposing tugging ropes.

This is when it gets fun.

The moment I walked into the room, the two of us instantly had some ropes from each of our spheres that connected to the ropes from the other person's sphere. The two of us are now a group; two spheres within a sphere.

That means if I get a little aggravated because it is too cool and walk over to turn up the thermostat, which makes my chair more stable, there is a good chance you will now feel some aggravation because it is too warm. At this point, you have a choice. You can think I purposefully turned the thermostat to aggravate you or you can think I inadvertently aggravated you by adjusting the thermostat. There is a HUGE difference between those two responses. Many of us are very tempted to think others are purposefully aggravating us rather than just blundering around seeking to end their own aggravations.

After years of trying to figure out group dynamics, my definition of "group" is a sphere of dialectical tensions.

If two of us are in the room, how many groups are there? Three—you have a sphere, I have a sphere, and our interconnected strings form another sphere.

If four people are in the room, there are 25 groups in the room. Actually, there are more than that because of those pesky Systemic Expectations that follow us wherever we go, but who is counting?

Has your jaw dropped yet? The math is factorial. If there are four people in the room, here is the formula: $(4 \times 3 \times 2) + 1$.

I used to think that ten people in the room was an easy group dynamic. I now conceptualize it is an incredibly complex interaction between 3,628,801 spheres (10 x 9 x 8 x 7 x 6 x 5 x 4 x 3 x 2)+1.

Go ahead, do the math to figure out how many groups are in a worship service with 100 people in the room.

Chapter 6—A Summary of the Challenges

To exist in unity, each group needs to determine which goals to pursue and what the plan is for that pursuit. There are at least five levels of goals. Most people do not even realize four of those levels exist, much less have the skill to figure out their own and others' goals on those levels. Due to adrenaline, most people react with damaging defensiveness rather than calm skill when they perceive, consciously or subconsciously, their goals are thwarted. Goals on all five levels are constantly changing. Each of us is constantly intertwined with a mind-boggling number of groups that cause us aggravation by yanking on our goal ropes. This is in a room full of people where every member is spiritually, physically, and mentally healthy. In reality, we are surrounded by a lot of people who, in one way or another, are not healthy. In short, unity (reaching 60% of a group's theoretical potential) requires miracles.

Remember, the main reason we spent so much time covering the principles in this chapter is so you will give yourself and others grace.

Part II—The Solutions

... until we all attain to the unity of the faith ... – Ephesians 4:13

As I type this sentence I am sitting in front of a captivating fire on a crisp fall day in the lodge at Discovery Ministries during their 35th Anniversary Celebration. How appropriate. The current staff and many of the former staff attending the celebration are the people who demonstrated great determination from 2005 to 2012 to do the hard work of learning, practicing and constantly refining the principles in this chapter. We read voraciously. We used ourselves as guinea pigs to figure out what works. Then we introduced the concepts into the groups we facilitated to ensure the principles worked in varied age groups and situations. Then we practiced more on ourselves. It was a wonderful learning cycle.

For instance, we studied and practiced effective meeting facilitation. For about five years, at the end of our weekly staff meetings we each completed an evaluation critiquing the facilitator, the meeting style, the meeting content, etc. It is challenging to have your facilitation evaluated by a bunch of facilitators.

The training pyramid below is my attempt to summarize what I learned while studying scripture, experimenting with the DM staff, training participants in the middle of adrenaline activities, and getting a Master's in Administration and Dispute Resolution. Notice each skill builds on all the skill(s) below it.

Unity

Effective Meetings

Accountability

Decide

Creative Thinking

Forgiveness

Speak the Truth in Love

Be Quick to Listen, Slow to Speak, and Slow to Anger

Love Your Neighbor as Yourself

Love God with All Your Heart, Soul, Mind, and Strength

Unity skills are like other adrenaline sport skills; they build on each other. No one would dream of putting a basketball player on the court in a college-level game who had never learned to dribble. It is crazy to take a novice whitewater canoer over a 10-foot drop before the person even knows how to make the canoe go straight. If I remember correctly, my sky diving instructor told me he could not teach me solo sky diving until I quit flailing around during the tandem dives. So why is it that we expect people to be productive contributors during important meetings before they know how to stay calm in disagreements, generally be friendly, effectively listen, speak the truth in love, and deal with offenses well?

The training pyramid is the outline for Part II. If you want to function in unity, you must master the basics. Please join me as we walk step-by-step through the solutions that transform us from muddling along to unity.

Chapter 7—Love the Lord your God

Love the Lord your God with all your heart, and with all your soul, and with all your mind, and with all your strength – Mark 12:30

Love God with All Your Heart, Soul, Mind, and Strength

The longer I facilitate and study unity, the more convinced I become that everything depends on getting as close as possible to completely loving Jesus. There are myriads of wonderful personal and corporate side effects of people falling deeply in love with Jesus. I am going to focus on one; peace that passes understanding.

It is easy to learn a few interpersonal conflict resolution principles. The challenge is performing them when all you want to do is win an argument or escape from the room. The fundamental challenge is the same with all adrenaline sports, controlling the "freak out" so you can do what you have trained to do.

A way to conceptualize the goal of peace that passes understanding is the following Graph:

The dashed line on the graph represents the point at which adrenaline kicks in for an individual, and a disagreement becomes a conflict. I believe it is possible to move your dashed line higher by getting closer to Jesus.

The closer you get to Jesus, the less circumstances make you freak out. Why?

You are a spirit. You temporarily live in a body. Picture a horse and rider that are attached together until the horse dies. The rider is the spirit—you. The horse is the body. To accomplish what you were put on this earth to do and be, you should be in control of your body. God designed your body with an instant warning system, adrenaline, that powerfully alerts you when a dangerous situation exists. When the rider is weak-willed and selfish, and the horse gets

39

spooked, the horse often goes crazy. It is a dangerous situation for the horse, the rider, and everyone in the vicinity. When the rider is strong-willed and loving, it is a different story because the rider has taken time to understand and train the horse to obey no matter how challenging the circumstance. When the horse of a strong-willed and loving rider gets spooked, the rider instantly senses it, evaluates the situation, and gives the horse instructions. The horse instantly obeys, and rather than being a danger to themselves and everyone around, this horse and rider spread "love, joy, peace, patience, kindness, goodness, faithfulness, gentleness, and self-control," Galatians 5:22-23, in challenging circumstances.

The closer people get to Jesus, the stronger and more loving they become, which enables them to control the body with greater ease.

There are many books written about getting closer to Jesus. Have fun reading them. I recommend the Bible.

In this section, we're going to focus on four practices that help you get closer to Jesus and stay calm during disagreements: effective breathing; prayer; scriptural meditation; and grounding your identity.

Effective Breathing

People cannot breathe well and freak out at the same time.

I was raised in a church that believed:

1. Meditation is evil.
2. Focused breathing is dangerously close to meditation.

If you have some of those same warnings in your mind, please finish reading this chapter before you decide whether or not I am a wolf in sheep's clothing.

Not long after beginning to instruct rappelling I noticed someone near the edge holding his breath. His whole body was shaking, and his face was turning red. I said, "Breathe." He did, laughed a little when he realized he had been holding his breath, then his entire body relaxed. The change was so dramatic, I took note and started watching for other people holding their breath. Sure enough, many people held their breaths at the edge of the cliff. Many others did just the opposite and started breathing too rapidly.

Once I became aware of this behavior, I noticed it at the top of the zipline, in the middle of rock climbing, in the middle of whitewater rapids, in tight spots in caves, during mediations, and anywhere else people were afraid.

Around that time Colette was leading a backpacking trip in the Wind River Range. She was pregnant (yes, she is that tough) and finding breathing a little more challenging than usual at high altitudes. Eugene Everson, an anesthetist in the group, told her your body receives oxygen and gets rid of carbon dioxide most efficiently if you inhale through your nose and exhale through pursed lips. She used the technique and found it very helpful. Colette passed the tip onto me, and it did not take long until I took a proactive approach. When I saw people getting nervous, I had them breathe in long and slowly through their noses and breathe out slowly through pursed lips. I asked them to focus on slowing and deepening their breaths. It is amazing. If people give in to fear, they stop breathing well; likewise, if people breathe well, fear has less grip. Less fear equals more effective thinking and acting.

According to Jeff Wise,[6] an investigative reporter, researchers have proven my observations, that breathing is a bridge between the reflective and the automatic elements in the brain because it can be controlled by both at the same time. The reflective part of the brain is the part that follows instructions. The automatic part is the part that screams, "AAAAAARRRRRRGH, I'm going to die!"

Let's go back to the horse and rider metaphor. The reflective part of the brain is the rider (or perhaps it is the decision-making tool of the rider. I am not trying to make a theological statement that the spirit is the reflective part of the brain. I am just trying to use an imperfect metaphor to describe unseen functions). The automatic part of the brain is the horse. When the horse freaks out, it is in control. When the rider breaths well, the rider is back in control.

Do you get the important training element? Train to make effective breathing your instant reaction to your body's adrenaline dump.

I am convinced Jesus designed breathing as the emergency switch our spirit can flip to regain control of the adrenaline filled body. That goes for physical adrenaline sports, challenging conversations with a spouse or children, intense moments in meetings, and standing on stage while people clap or boo.

When I first started trying to overcome my natural reactions, I trained to instantly breathe well. It helped quite a bit. Breathing well made it so I could instantly start doing what I know I should do, rather than allowing my body, mainly my mind and mouth, to do what it wants to do.

Which brings up a good point. You just breathed well. You, spirit, are in control. Now what?

Prayer

Let's continue with the horse and rider metaphor. You are a spirit, the rider. You were never created to be the Lone Ranger. You were created to ride so close to Jesus, the Master Horseman who created you and your horse, that you can clearly hear and obey His instructions and hand Him the reins to your horse.

You can also ignore Jesus and keep the reins in your own control, that is freewill.

Prayer allows Jesus to control you just as breathing allows you to control your horse. While you are praying effectively, Jesus has your full attention and the reins to your horse. Philippians 4:6-7 states, "Be anxious for nothing, but in everything by prayer and supplication with thanksgiving let your requests be made known to God. And the peace of God, which surpasses all comprehension, will guard your hearts and your minds in Christ Jesus." 1 Thessalonians 5:17 states, "pray without ceasing." Again, in Ephesians 6:18 we are advised, "With all prayer and petition pray at all times in the Spirit." Do you get it? The key to staying focused on eternal realities is to pray.

If your concept of praying is folding your hands and closing your eyes at mealtimes, you have an opportunity to abundantly expand your prayer life. If you are supposed to pray without ceasing, how can you pray with your eyes closed? If you are supposed to pray without ceasing, how can you keep your hands on the steering wheel while they are neatly folded in your lap? Have you ever thought of anxiety as an indicator that you need to pray? It is beyond the scope of this book to train all the facets of prayer. Frankly, I still have a lot to learn.

As I gained experience and skill, and started praying early and often during challenges, I noticed a dramatic increase in my ability to stay calm. I still mess up, because I still live in this crazy world. However, my wife tells me there is a night and day difference between my actions and reactions ten years ago and now that is not due to getting older.

I hope you are now convinced you need to breathe and pray effectively. Perhaps you are wondering what to pray when under duress. Might I recommend praying scripture? How about getting really wild and mix prayer and scriptural meditation so much that it is hard to tell one from the other?

Scriptural Meditation

Years ago, I was mountain biking with Chris, one of our interns at DM. I was a decent mountain biker, meaning I didn't often fall off my bike. He was an excellent mountain biker, meaning he did well competing in races. We came to a typical Ozark Mountain old logging road that dropped steeply into the hollow (pronounced holler), had a base layer of loose gravel, and a plethora of logs and small-child-sized boulders scattered in menacing patterns. Chris plunged down the hill at breakneck speed and made it to the bottom without hitting anything. I, on the other hand, tried to take a few layers off my brake pads, and introduced my front tire to several logs and rocks along the way. I did not fall. I just had to put my foot down several times and move the bike over to a manageable path. Chris waited for me at the bottom.

When I made it to him, I asked, "How did you do that?"

"Do what?" He replied.

"You went down that steep maze fast and didn't hit anything. I went slow and felt like I was in a pinball machine."

"It's simple." Chris kindly lectured. "I look where I want to go, and you look at what you want to miss."

I showed my keen intellect when I responded, "Huh?"

Chris patiently expounded, "If you will focus 20 feet in front of your bike and trace with your eye the route you want to take, that is the route your bike will follow. I look where I want my bike to go. You are probably looking a few feet in front of your front tire, and focusing on the rocks and trees you want to miss. Your bike goes where you look and focus."

That information revolutionized my bike riding. I also applied it to driving and whitewater canoeing. It works. The vehicle goes where the eye looks. Perhaps this explains why law-abiding citizens run over stationary patrol cars, lit up with pretty lights, at the side of the road.

A year or so later, I was sitting around a campfire with a backpacking group. We were trying to figure out why memorizing scripture makes such a big difference in our lives. They were interested because I had required them to memorize at least one verse per day for seven days, and they were convinced the memory work was influencing their behavior. I knew it did. I made the group memorize scripture simply because I knew that for some reason I found it easier to live like Jesus while I was memorizing scripture. However, before that debriefing I could not explain why. During the debriefing, someone mentioned Psalm 119:11, "Your word have I treasured in my heart, that I may not sin against You." In that moment Chris's mountain biking lesson, and a sermon I heard years earlier, came together for me.

I excitedly told the group the following, and they agreed we had stumbled on why memorizing scripture works. The pastor years earlier said the word for sin in Psalm 119:11 is an archery term that means "to miss the target." I also told the group what Chris taught me while we were mountain biking. If you do not miss a target, what do you do? You hit the target. Life has this in common with archery and mountain biking. You have the choice to focus on what you want to do and be, or to focus on all the bad attitudes and situations that hinder abundant life. You hit where you focus. Memorizing scripture puts the pictures in your mind of the path you want to hit.

I got excited a couple of years after that backpacking discussion when I read Goddard and Neumann's rock climbing training manual[7] and found out researchers have proven picturing a movement in your mind is the foundational step to doing the movement.

Let me give you a practical example of this principle in action. Unfortunately, I began cussing in sixth grade because I wanted to be cool and fit in with the other kids. Cussing is an insidious habit that interferes with abundant living. When I was sixteen, I felt strongly that Jesus wanted me to stop cussing, so, I tried to stop. Imagine with me that "trop" is a cuss word. I often prayed, "Jesus, please help me to quit saying 'trop.'" What was I focused on? If you answered, "trop," you are correct. After debriefing with the backpacking group, I quit trying to stop cussing. Instead, I memorized Ephesians 4:15 and 29, James 1:19-20, and similar verses. When pressure built, I quoted those verses, and aimed at speaking and thinking well. It was a big day in my life a few years later when I smashed my thumb with a hammer and thought and said, "Ouch!" I suspect Colette thought I was crazy when I ran upstairs and joyfully told her I smashed my thumb with a hammer.

Scriptural meditation depends on the first piece of the full armor of God mentioned in Ephesians 6:14: Truth! Truth is the foundation of standing firm in this life. When the Bible talks about meditating (Joshua 1:8, Psalm 1:2, Psalm 4:4, etc.), it means running through your mind over and over the truth that scripture teaches and discovering the depths of its meaning and application in your life. I like the way Selwyn Hughes described meditating, "It involves taking a phrase or verse from the Word of God, the Bible, and thinking about it until it begins to affect every area of your life. In a sense, meditation is really the digestion system of the soul" (p. 67).[8] The most effective way to do this is memorizing scripture. Even memorizing and chewing on one verse is beneficial. I have found it helpful to memorize verses that deal with my current struggles. The more you memorize, the better you aim. The better you aim, the more you live like Jesus, benefiting yourself, those around you, and the Kingdom. The more you memorize, the easier it gets to memorize. Please, I beg you, learn and apply scripture.

Remember, the reason we are digging into breathing, prayer, and scriptural meditation is all the unity skills build on the peace that comes from abiding with Jesus.

There is a final practice I recommend that helps you live in peace that passes understanding.

Ground Your Identity

Hopefully, the word "identity" reminds you of the (**RIPS**) we discussed in chapter 2. Remember those recipe cards that are written in invisible ink that only your adrenaline can read? Let's learn why and how to make the ink visible on a conscious level.

For 22 years I have trained people in teamwork. The first ten years I started summarizing the training with "love your neighbor as yourself." I would tell groups, "I know that is the second greatest commandment. I know the greatest is to love God. I am just not sure how, on a practical level, loving God affects teamwork."

Then I read about grounding your identity in <u>Difficult Conversations</u>.[9] The authors state that grounding your identity, having a more accurate view of yourself, makes you less defensive during disagreements.

Perhaps that was the biggest "Aha" moment of my life. I got excited! It made sense why Romans 12:3, about having accurate understanding of self, lays the foundation for the rest of that great teamwork chapter. The principles about effective breathing, prayer, and scriptural meditation instantly came together in my mind as part of a foundational training regimen for all the other teamwork skills. The closer people get to Jesus, the more accurately they understand who He created them to be, which makes people healthy.

The performance of the group depends on the health of each person in the group; as Paul writes in Ephesians 4:16, "according to the proper working of each individual part." Parts only work well when they function as The Creator intended.

In their book, Stone, Patton, and Heen give two tips about grounding your identity. First, recognize the identity. Remember the recipe cards that are written in invisible ink? Just realizing that I have a certain identity card in my recipe box makes the ink on that card visible, and there is less need to defend the identity.

Admitting to myself that I have an identity is easier said than done. The staff at DM studied, then practiced this principle. We concluded when a person gets upset during a conversation, that person is, more than likely, defending an unknown identity. We began viewing getting upset as an indicator for identity work, much like warning lights on the car are vital for getting the car fixed. When I get upset, I realize I need to spend time with Jesus, and maybe a close friend who is skilled at facilitative listening, to figure out what identities I am defending that I do not yet realize I have in my recipe box. Realizing an identity brings release. Once it is realized, it is much less likely to cause me to get upset. I have not tried to understand this phenomenon, I just know it works.

Once you realize an identity, you are ready for step two, which takes the flame out of an identity—complexify it.

If I sing a solo during worship and afterwards overhear someone say, "That soloist was much better after I turned off my hearing aid." I get upset, go home, and realize I have an identity card in my recipe box that reads, "I am a good singer." I can re-write that card so it more accurately reflects reality and makes it so I have nothing to defend. Something like this:

> I like to sing. Many people say I sing well. Some days I sing better than others due to stress, illness, or other challenges. People might not like my singing because they don't like the genre I am singing, or they are comparing me to a singer with a completely different tone. I like some singers and not others, and they are all skilled singers. I have been selected in some auditions and not selected in others. People might not like my singing because the sound system level or other elements of the venue are annoying them.

Now I can hear a comment like, "That soloist was much better after I turned off my hearing aid." without getting upset because there is lots of room in that identity for the other person's experience and opinion. Several of us at DM found it helpful to get out a piece of paper and write a realized identity with the complexifying statements. After I realize and complexify an identity, it almost disappears.

Take the identity grounding theory a step farther. What if it was possible to have such an accurate view of yourself and the world that the only identity you cling to is Jesus created and loves me? Imagine the freedom! No one can threaten or take that away from you. Can you imagine interacting with people without feeling the need to impress them, or defend yourself; without feeling overwhelmed by the desire to speak your mind or escape out of the room? Even if this was the only element—I think there are many more—of freedom that Jesus offers, it would be a miraculous life. When I made the connection between the greatest commandment and grounding your identity, John 8:31-32 lept off the page at me, "So Jesus was saying to those Jews who had believed Him, 'If you continue in My word, then you are truly disciples of mine; and you will know the truth, and the truth will make you free.'" Scripture is full of that promise. Any other identity that you or I cling to is a chain that binds because it makes us vulnerable to hurt when interacting with others.

Let me pull all the concepts in this book to this point together for you.

Imagine that you are riding in a car with me before I learned and practiced any of these concepts. We are going along having a fascinating conversation about Christianity when all of a sudden a car passes by your window in a blur, pulls in front of us, misses our bumper by a couple of feet and continues wildly weaving through traffic. You are shocked as the interesting person beside you instantly transforms into Dr. Jekyll. An expletive flies from my mouth, my body tenses, and my face turns red as I: hit the brake hard almost causing the car behind to hit us; describe, in unflattering terms, the person who narrowly missed us; and make harsh recommendations for how society should deal with reckless drivers.

Now imagine that you are riding in a car with me today. Same conversation. Same car passes in a blur. You hear me inhale through my nose, exhale through my mouth and say, "You, O LORD, are a shield about me, my glory, and the one who lifts my head." You look over and notice I am scanning the mirrors with my foot off the gas. You hear me breathe once more through my nose and out my mouth. Then I say, "Father, I am not sure what is happening with the driver of that car. Please protect him and everyone else on the road physically, spiritually, and emotionally."

You may think I am exaggerating, but I have witnesses; my wife and children can attest to the difference in my driving. I am not consistent. Some days the harsh thoughts come first, but they rarely get past the point of inception to make it out of my mouth. Praise God! He changes people! The principles work!

I asked one of my daughters if I can write the previous paragraph with integrity. She said, "It works when you are already in a good mood. When you are in a bad mood, sometimes you still slip." What can I say? I have a ways to go.

You want a challenging thought? Your response if you were driving the car is probably how you respond during challenging conversations and meetings. You might better control the visible and audible elements of your reactions when people are around, but the internal elements are similar.

The communication reality is most people are experts, at a sub-conscious level, at reading non-verbal body language. Since our body language accurately conveys our thoughts, the painful reality is every thought a person thinks affects everyone else in the room. Have you ever walked into a room and felt the tension in the room even though no one was speaking? What you experienced was your sub-conscious read of all the body language.

Unity depends on people abiding in peace that passes understanding, and giving each other grace as we go through this incredibly complicated and crazy world together.

Now we get to talk about the stuff that is easier to conceptualize and practice.

Chapter 8—Love Your Neighbor As Yourself

"You shall love your neighbor as yourself." There is no other commandment greater than these. – Mark 12:31

Love Your Neighbor as Yourself
Love God with All Your Heart, Soul, Mind, and Strength

In Mark 12:31 Jesus tells us we are to love people. In Matthew 7:12, toward the end of the Sermon on the Mount, He gives great insight into how to love people. He states The Golden Rule, "In everything, therefore, treat people the same way you want them to treat you, for this is the Law and the Prophets." The Golden Rule is easy to state, and very challenging to apply. Let me explain.

Imagine with me, if you will, that I like chocolate bars, you dislike chocolate bars, you like gummy bears, and I dislike gummy bears. When we meet, I want to give you something you will enjoy. I know the Golden Rule, so I give you a chocolate bar.

Did I love you well? I treated you the same way I want to be treated. This is the way most of us walk around practicing love.

What if our encounter went more like this:

    Me: "Hi. I have a chocolate bar and gummy bears.

        Which do you prefer?"

    You: "I like gummy bears."

    I hand you gummy bears.

You can see the difference between the two encounters. Love requires getting to know people and treating them how they would want to be treated. This gets tricky when the other person has a bad habit and wants you to support that habit, because participating in another person's destructive behavior is not love. My current favorite definition of love is M. Scott Peck's.[10] He asserts that love is the effort I make to support my eternally beneficial growth and the eternally beneficial growth of every person I meet.

How to love a person who refuses to quit harmful behaviors is beyond the scope of this book. The relationships section of Henry Cloud's Necessary Endings[11] is a good book to start learning that skill.

Many tools provide shortcuts to understanding people around you. At Discovery Ministries we created a book that contained each person's Myers-Briggs Type,[12] conflict style,[5] and love language.[13] Whoever needed to have a challenging conversation with another person could consult the book to figure out the best way to approach the person.

Do whatever it takes. Love requires learning about other people.

A word of caution: if you ever think you have yourself, anyone else, or any situation completely figured out, you need to get help until you realize you are not God. This caution is what corrected my false identity—"I am right!"—so I could finally start comprehending and practicing the principles in this book. We will talk more on this in the next section of the book when we discuss the tentative opening of listening.

On a very practical level, I conceptualize loving those around me as maintaining a positive emotional bank account with them. Covey[14] introduced me to this concept, stating that if I have a positive emotional bank account with you, then you are probably comfortable interacting with me and might allow me to influence your life. If I have a negative account with you, then you do not want to be around me, much less want me to influence you.

Let me illustrate this principle with one of the most important unity withdrawals and deposits: advice and encouragement. I first noticed the power of advice and encouragement while watching groups go through the low obstacle course at DM. The obstacles are about one foot off the ground. Participants attempt the challenges, one at a time, while six people surround them to help them hit the ground well if they fall. The course is scary and exciting—for the participant. The rest of the group struggles to stay awake because they must walk slowly, and hold their hands at-the-ready, as they watch the same slow event for the hundredth time.

I did not notice the difference between advice and encouragement until I became interested in why groups would have fun and lots of energy in some moments yet struggle through drudgery in other moments. There were few groups who had all fun, or all drudgery. For most, it came in waves. Through a couple of years of observation and post-event discussions, I concluded the event tends toward drudgery when people shout advice at each other. It tends toward fun and energy when people shout encouragement. Further, I concluded that advice is a withdrawal from the emotional bank account of five while encouragement is a deposit of one. There is evidence to support this ratio.[15]

The groups also helped me define advice and encouragement.

1. Advice—pointing out what I think people should do.
2. Encouragement—pointing out what people are doing well, or what they are doing that I appreciate.

After I realized the definitions of advice and encouragement, and their effects on emotional bank accounts, I asked the following questions to hundreds of groups, and consistently received the following answers.

1. When do you like unsolicited advice? Hardly ever.
2. When do you like encouragement? Almost always.
3. What do you do when you see people struggling? Give them advice.

Here is the related question I began asking every group of teenagers. Why don't you listen to your parents? The universal answer—because they are constantly telling me what to do.

Do employees ignore their bosses for the same reason? Is it possible unsolicited advice might be the single most damaging attack on unity?

Advice says that I am smarter than you, and can better accomplish what you are doing. No one wants to hear that! Even asked-for-advice becomes a withdrawal of five after 30 seconds, with further withdrawal of five every 30 seconds the barrage of knowledge continues.

Do we need to give each other advice in life? Absolutely. The challenge is to make sure I have a substantial emotional bank account with the people I am advising, so they can hear the advice, still want to be around me, and still be influenced by me. That means I must point out what they are doing well at least five times more often than I give advice.

Granted, there are other deposits and withdrawals. I view the Five Love Languages as ways to make emotional bank account deposits:

1. Words of Affirmation.
2. Touch.
3. Gifts.
4. Acts of Service.
5. Time Spent.[13]

During the Joplin Tornado relief, we strategized how to bolster the seven main leaders in the distribution system. We figured out a quick way to make deposits with all five love languages. As we walked up, we smiled and said, "Thank you for doing _____ so well. That element of your area is really running smoothly." (words of affirmation). We then gave them a bottle of water and a choice of snack (gifts). Then, after getting permission, we massaged their shoulders while praying for them for a few moments (touch, acts of service, time spent). You may argue that a 30-second prayer is not long enough to be "time spent," but given the crush of responsibility and the fast pace of those first few days, 30-seconds indeed seemed like a long and precious time.

Each person has their own list of deposits and withdrawals. Most people have a hard time communicating what is on their lists, and their lists change over time. I didn't say it was easy to maintain a positive emotional bank account, only necessary. I focus on encouragement, words of affirmation, because it seems to be on every person's list.

I will never forget the electrifying "Aha!" moment I finally grasped the relationship between:

1. Advice vs. encouragement.
2. Your body does what you picture in your mind.[7]

I was working with a high school girls' volleyball team. We talked about the slumps that happen in volleyball games. Can a team do anything to combat the slumps? I asked what they do when someone makes a bad hit. They agreed they most often slapped each other on the rump and said, "Shake it off!"

That was when it dawned on me, and I excitedly asked, "What is 'it'?" At first, they looked at me like I had three heads. After I explained the two principles, we all got excited as we figured out "it" is the bad hit. They realized when they said, "Shake it off!" they were:

1. Giving unasked for advice, which was subconsciously getting them annoyed with one another.
2. Putting pictures in their minds of what they did *not* want to happen.

They thought for a while and came up with a solution. They determined that if someone made a bad hit, those around would immediately say something like, "I want to see a great hit like you did two plays ago." They became determined to give encouragement that only put positive pictures in their minds.

They were state champions that year. The team had a lot going for them before I worked with them; however, I asked a couple of players if the encouragement made a difference. Their eyes lit up as they excitedly told me that the team believed it made a *huge* difference. They did run into an unexpected challenge. They quickly figured out that shouting, "Shake it off!" was such a deeply ingrained habit that the players on the court could not refrain; so, the bench took the responsibility of specific encouragement. Undoing bad habits is not a quick process, and we all need to look out for each other.

Did I mention that training and determination to give specific encouragement, rather than advice, revolutionized my marriage, parenting, and professional life!?

There is another skill that is vital for loving people and making deposits in emotional bank accounts.

Chapter 9—Be Quick to Listen, Slow to Speak, and Slow to Anger

This you know, my beloved brethren. But everyone must be quick to hear, slow to speak and slow to anger; for the anger of man does not achieve the righteousness of God. – James 1:19-20

Be Quick to Listen, Slow to Speak, and Slow to Anger
Love Your Neighbor as Yourself
Love God with All Your Heart, Soul, Mind, and Strength

After writing the previous section I asked my wife, "What had more positive impact in our marriage: my learning to give encouragement or learning to listen?" She thought for a moment, then said, "Listen."

Years ago, my daughters were driving me nuts. At the time, they were ages six, four, and one. Consistently, we would get in the car or sit at the table, and they would all talk at once. The volume steadily rose until I needed ear plugs. I was convinced I needed to train them to be quiet. I had just started praying to God for a solution to this training challenge, when I read a principle that brought peace to my family.

Let me preface by telling you that I had been trying to learn to listen for ten years. I first recognized the need to develop listening skills about the second year I led team training activities. I noticed that in most groups, multiple people talked at the same time while strategizing solutions and tackling challenges. During debriefings I asked, "How many people were talking at the same time?" People would quickly recognize that most of the time during the challenge, multiple people talked simultaneously. Next, I asked, "How many people can talk at once in order for the group to communicate effectively?"

I even tried a little experiment with people who thought they could listen to more than one person simultaneously. I would have them stand between two people. I gave each of the two a simple five-word sentence to say. The two sentences were different. On the count of three, each of the two said their sentence at the same time, then I asked the people in the middle to repeat the two sentences. Not one person could repeat back all ten simple words. There was no trick; I told everyone ahead of time exactly how the experiment would go. In that simple controlled environment, with plenty of time to prepare, no one could listen to more than one person. Even if there are people who could repeat the ten words, I doubt they could repeat back the words of more than one speaker under normal daily listening conditions.

Eventually, I narrowed the debriefings to the following questions, and consistently received the following answers.

1. When you talk what do you want others to do? *Listen.*

2. What do you mean by listen? *While I am trying to describe the picture that is on the canvas in my mind, I want you to concentrate on drawing that picture on the canvas in your mind.*

3. When someone else is talking and you disagree with that person, what are you doing in your head? *I am building arguments to prove my point and watching for an opportunity to cut in on the other person to make those points.*

Listening requires setting my thoughts aside to concentrate on your thoughts.

The lack of listening is a foundational challenge to group function.

A few months after I came to this conclusion, I attended a facilitation conference. I sat at a lunch table with a woman visiting the U.S.A. from New Zealand. In the middle of the interesting conversation, someone asked her, "What was the first thing you noticed that is different in America?"

She thought for a moment, then replied, "You know, the first thing I noticed is how loud Americans are.

They constantly speak their ideas and are always interrupting each . . ."

At that moment I excitedly said, "I know what you mean. I have noticed the same thing!"

She sat back, laughed, and said, "See what I mean?"

I interrupted her because I could not wait to tell what I was learning in debriefings about listening. I don't know whether to laugh or cry about the irony of that moment. It was poignant and painful to me. I wish I could say I went away from that encounter skilled at listening. I did not. I went away realizing I needed to learn how to listen.

A couple of years later, I was a participant on a 16-day wilderness challenge trip. Every person in the group had a strong personality, which made for difficult communication. The conversations rarely contained rude remarks, but every person had an opinion and an extreme urge to share it. The first day we realized how often we interrupted each other, and that we needed to be more respectful. Even so, we still frequently interrupted each other throughout the trip. I became extremely frustrated trying to share ideas until finally, on day 11, I experimented with being silent. I decided not to speak except to point out what someone was doing that I appreciated or to answer a direct question. From this experiment, I learned six valuable points that I recorded in my trip journal.

1. I have an opinion about virtually everything, yet my opinion is rarely needed.
2. If I always give an opinion, everyone learns to block out what I say, so that they do not listen when I have an opinion that does matter.
3. I have less stress when I am purposefully silent, because I do not have to compete with everyone else to voice my opinion.
4. For the first time in my life, I am listening well. It is much easier to focus on what someone else is saying when I am not just waiting for a break in their thought so I can interject mine.
5. When I am silent, I do not start resenting others for not listening to me.
6. In a group, most of my opinions are eventually spoken by someone else.

For a few weeks after that trip, I listened well, then I easily slipped back into old habits; until . . .

I was praying for a solution to tame my children's tongues when I read that when people do not feel heard, they often repeat themselves, and often get louder with each repetition.[16] Ouch! My children were rude and loud because their daddy was not listening.

I was determined to experiment. I quickly learned rudimentary listening skills from Wilmot and Hocker,[17] then waited for my opportunity. It came quickly. That afternoon we were getting in the car when Kiersten, the four-year-old, said, "Daddy look at my doll." I was ready! I said, "Honey, it sounds like you are excited about your beautiful doll!" She said, "Yes!" and quietly sat down in her seat. I danced a little jig outside the car, and became determined to learn listening. Since that day, our home and car rides have been filled with content quiet.

Don't get me wrong, I didn't instantly get skilled at listening. Reading that book was the first time I realized that listening is an adrenaline skill—just as much as white water paddling—and requires training just like any other adrenaline sport. That experience with my daughter happened in the fall of 2005. While I was dancing the jig outside my car, I realized I also needed to learn to listen to everyone else in my life.

After that success with Kiersten, I began to apply what I knew about adrenaline sport training to the listening models I studied. From that point forward, I got better and better at listening. Every inch of progress made noticeable positive difference in my interactions at home, work, and church.

I quickly came to view listening as *the* teamwork skill to practice in order to develop all other unity skills. As a beginner in white water paddling, instructors told me the quickest way to gain overall proficiency was to improve the forward stroke. At first, I thought that sounded boring and crazy. I soon realized their wisdom. Although the forward stroke looks simple, it is almost impossible to do perfectly every time. The only way to make progress on the forward stroke is to improve all paddling basics. Even now, after 20 years, if I want to improve any facet of paddling, I work on my forward stroke. Listening is the same way. It is almost impossible to be a perfect listener. Yet, working on listening will improve all your other unity skills.

My experience personally and corporately is the more skill each group member has in listening, the easier it is to move toward unity. Think about it. Listening requires me to focus on what the other person is communicating, which requires me to set my thoughts aside, which requires me to stay calm, which requires me to control my adrenaline and thoughts. A room full of calm focused people is a great foundation for unity.

There are many classes and trainings that teach the basic listening formula. People commonly leave those classes, try out the formula on others, get a response something like, "Don't use that listening crap on me." and never try using the formula again. That is because wielding the formula without underlying love and respect comes across as manipulation. Remember, loving God and people needs to come first.

71

Equipping Ministries International (EMI) has a good model for learning listening (See Appendix A)[18]. The basic elements of listening are: tentative opening; name the emotion(s); connector word; and rephrase/reframe.

Tentative Opening

I laughed so hard when I wrote this in the Love-Your-Neighbor-section, that I am going to write it again. "If you ever think you have yourself, anyone else, or any situation completely figured out, you need to get help until you realize you are not GOD."

A tentative opening, spoken honestly and respectfully, quickly conveys, "I am doing my best to understand you and the situation, and I realize my attempts are error-prone." Here are some examples of tentative openings.

1. So. . . .
2. If I hear you correctly. . . .
3. I'm not sure I'm following. . . .
4. Am I hearing you say. . . .
5. Let me see if I understand. . . .

Remember, the wording isn't that important; however, the attitude behind the wording is vital.

Name the Feeling(s)

After the tentative opening, you name the feeling. When done lovingly and respectfully, this works miracles. The more intense a feeling is, the more it tends to act as plugs in the ear canals. This may not seem important, until you remember that people repeat themselves louder and louder until they feel heard. The main way to confirm you heard them is by speaking their thoughts back to them. If their ears are plugged, they cannot hear what you are saying. First you must unplug their ears; somehow, respectfully naming an emotion says to a person that it is valid to feel the emotion, which allows the emotion to exist calmly rather than intensely. Thus, it quits plugging their ears.

It is more complicated, but we do not need to know the science to wield the tool.

Interestingly, you do not necessarily need to correctly name the emotion. Many times when I name the incorrect emotions, the other people say, "No. I feel . . ." Hooray! I just helped them validate their own emotions, and it still has the same calming effect.

There are many people, especially in a business setting, who will tune you out if you use the words "you feel." In those places say, "You are . . ." If I am unsure, I err on the side of not using the word "feel." So, instead of saying, "You feel uncertain." I would say, "You are uncertain."

If the level of emotion is low in a conversation, you can skip the step of naming the emotion(s).

I had about eight emotion words in my vocabulary before I learned about listening. The EMI listening sheet (Appendix A) lists 175 emotion words,[18 above] and arranges them from low to high levels of intensity. I made my own list of about 100 words in the following categories: mad, sad, glad, afraid, confused, ashamed, lonely, confident, accomplished, joyful. There are a *lot* of emotions.

Connector Word

You need to use a connector word—and, because, when, or about—to make your emotion(s) identification flow into the next listening element. This will make more sense when we look at examples.

Rephrase or Reframe

Rephrasing is repeating back, in your own words, the essence of what the person said. For instance, if you said, "What is that horrible smell?" I could rephrase, "What stinks?"

Reframing is more challenging. Remember the iceberg acronym **TRIPS** (Chapter 2 - Tangible, Role/Relationship, Identity, Process, Systemic Expectations)? To reframe, you pick the **TRIPS** interest(s) out of what the person said, and

74

state them back in a way that points toward making the future better. It is challenging for me to give a reframing example without using the whole formula.

You say, "What is that horrible smell?"

My rephrase might be, "It sounds like (tentative opening) you are puzzled (emotion) because (connector) something stinks (rephrase).

My reframe might be, "It sounds like (same tentative opening) you are puzzled (emotion) and (connector) would like to get rid of that smell."

Notice the rephrase simply repeats the thought. The reframe puts a picture in your mind of the interest you want to accomplish.

You say, "You are such an idiot! How could you forget to make coffee for the meeting!?"

My rephrase—after I breath in through my nose and out through my lips, and remember to stay calm—might be, "So (tentative opening), you are outraged (feeling) that (connector) we do not have coffee." Notice, I acknowledged the challenge, yet I did not accept the blame.

My reframe—after remaining calm—might be, "So (tentative opening), you are outraged (feeling) and (connector) would like to ensure we have coffee for all future meetings?" Of course, this answer assumes it was not clear who was supposed to provide coffee for the meeting. If it was clearly my job to provide coffee for the meeting that last phrase would have been, "and you would like me to immediately get coffee for this meeting and give you my plan for ensuring this never happens again?"

Rephrasing is fairly easy to learn, and is helpful.

Reframing is an advanced skill that is science and art. When you effectively reframe for people, you give them the gift of helping them realize their **TRIPS** interests, and make the current challenge seem doable. In short, you bring clarity and hope into the situation.

When a group is trying to figure out a solution to a challenge, people's **TRIPS** interests are like jigsaw puzzle pieces in their pockets. Many times they do not realize they have those puzzle pieces in their pockets. One person in the room who is skilled in reframing can help the entire group get all the jigsaw puzzle pieces on the table. When all the pieces are on the table, the group can design a more complete solution.

Is it worth the effort to learn how to help people get all the goals on the table so they can craft complete solutions? Yes! Listening is vital to unity!

Chapter 10—Speak the Truth in Love

But speaking the truth in love, we are to grow up in all aspects into Him who is the head, even Christ. . . . – Ephesians 4:15

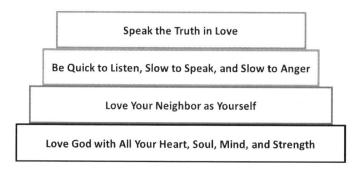

Words are like fire—they can bring warmth and comfort, or be a destructive force destroying everything in their path. Glass blowers, and other fire users, diligently study and practice principles to skillfully wield fire. In the same way, we who crave unity must train to skillfully wield words. Two main facets of speaking the truth in love are: tame the lions and get interests on the table.

Tame the Lions

First, do no harm. A couple of years ago, I thought of a word picture to describe the training progressions I have gone through to tame my tongue. Taming my tongue is like taming lions in a cage at a circus. The lion cage is my mind.

The lions are the thoughts in my mind. My efforts to filter my thoughts before they leave my mouth are like a lion tamer standing in front of an open cage door to prevent any lions from getting out the door to attack the crowd.

In my early years, there was not a lion tamer in the cage. Sarcasm, feelings of superiority, witty comments, and verbal domination pervade my family tree. Many iconic stories my grandmother told me about her family included a sense of pride about the bull-headed confrontational skills of my ancestors. I came by it honestly. Growing up, I often said things I regretted, felt horrible and awkward about them, then blundered on my merry way not knowing how to change.

In my 20's I encountered scriptures and situations that convinced me I needed to control my mouth. Here are three of the main scriptures.

1. Like a madman who throws firebrands, arrows and death, so is the man who deceives his neighbor, and says, "Was I not joking?" – Proverbs 26:18-19

2. Let no unwholesome word proceed from your mouth, but only such a word as is good for edification according to the need of the moment, so that it will give grace to those who hear. – Ephesians 4:29

78

3. Let not many of you become teachers, my brethren, knowing that as such we will incur a stricter judgment. For we all stumble in many ways. If anyone does not stumble in what he says, he is a perfect man, able to bridle the whole body as well. – James 3:1-2

I also encountered several similar situations as an instructor at DM, and in my home, that convinced me I had to tame the lions. Someone acted dangerously, then I said a sarcastic reprimand, then the person kept doing the action because she thought I was joking. The instructors at DM helped me realize people often could not tell whether I was being serious or joking. That is a *serious* problem when I am responsible for other people's training and safety.

My first progress in taming the lions in my mind was learning some principles I used as filters between my brain and my mouth. To continue the metaphor, it was like learning how to use a whip and chair, and stepping in the lion cage to keep the lions from getting out the door. These are common principles you can find in most interpersonal communication books and trainings.

1. If you want to criticize or correct, speak to the person in private. Do not talk about him while he is not in the room.

2. If you have praise to convey, speak about the person all you want anywhere you want.

3. Ask permission before sharing another person's story.

4. Describe your perspective. Use ownership language. Here are some examples.

    a. "This is what I see, hear, smell, taste, feel . . ."

    b. "From my perspective . . ."

    c. "My opinion is . . ."

5. Use accurate adverbs: often, sometimes, frequently, etc.

6. Avoid inaccurate adverbs, especially next to "you." Here are some classics to avoid because they are like gasoline and a lit match.

    a. "You always . . ."

    b. "You never . . ."

7. Avoid "you make me . . ." Each of us chooses our attitudes and actions. Yes, a captor or abuser can use physical abuse or torture to control my actions. Even then, I choose my attitudes and responses to situations and emotions.

The summary of these principles is "speak the truth in love." LaFasto and Larson call this openness and supportiveness—speaking all the pertinent interests with respect for others.[19]

Let me illustrate.

My wife, Colette, and I have an agreement that my desk is my space. Things on and in my desk may only be used with my permission and should be put right back. I realize at this point you might be thinking my wife has a jerk for a husband. That is not true. I am a recovering jerk. Regardless, there is a long history behind that agreement. It is the result of a few collaborative dialogs, and we are both still satisfied with the solution.

Now, let's assume I walk in the house after a day of work, walk into the kitchen, and notice my stapler on the kitchen counter surrounded by all sorts of random household items. The foolish thing is to yell at the top of my lungs, so all in the house hear, "Who took my stapler!? Colette, you make me so mad! You took my stapler from my desk without asking, and it is at severe risk of being lost in the mess you and the girls created!" This kind of response is like many lions getting loose in my house. When I speak in this way my children want to run and hide, and Colette feels obligated to protect them by saying something like, "Put away your own stupid stapler!"

The wiser thing is to find Colette, get in a private place, and quietly say to her, "Colette, I see my stapler on the counter. You *usually* put my supplies right back on my desk. Is everything OK?" Notice I spoke my irrefutable truth. I do see the stapler on the counter, there is nothing to debate in that sentence. I also spoke only to the person involved. I also acknowledged that she is a competent person. Finally, the follow up question wraps that truth in love because it assumes that she would keep our agreement unless circumstances were hard. This makes it easier for Colette to say, "I know the stapler is on the counter. I agree I should have put it back. As I was walking to put it back one of the girls screamed a blood curdling scream that indicated severe injury. I dropped the stapler and ran downstairs. After wiping up the blood, bandaging the wound, and mediating the argument that led to the injury, I realized it was time to fix supper. Somewhere in there, I forgot about the stapler. I deeply appreciate your concern for the girls and me, and I love you."

Do you see how speaking the truth in love made it easier for me to gladly put away my own stapler, and the family to sit down and have an enjoyable dinner? There are rewards for taming the lions.

Let's carry the lion-tamer metaphor a bit farther. The closer I got to Jesus and the more skill I gained in communication, the more I realized lions in the cage affect the crowd. People are experts, on a subconscious level, at reading non-verbal body language.[20] That means my thoughts, even when they don't leave my mouth, affect the

82

people around me. I came to this conclusion long before I read research about it. I watched group after group be affected by frowns, crossed arms, rolling eyes, smiles, and other actions of group members. I experimented, and soon realized I could influence the group just by smiling or frowning. I soon realized my determination to stay mentally present and supportive really boiled down to controlling my thoughts.

The only way I can communicate truth in love is for truth in love to permeate my thoughts. The ultimate solution is to get rid of the lions. This is where I now focus most of my efforts. Rather than trying to tame lions, I now do what Philippians 4:8 recommends for replacing the lions.

> Finally, brethren, whatever is true, whatever is honorable, whatever is right, whatever is pure, whatever is lovely, whatever is of good repute, if there is any excellence and if anything worthy of praise, dwell on these things.

Refer to Chapter 7 for a refresher on controlling your thoughts.

Are my thoughts perfect? No; however, they are healthier than ever and continue getting better. My wife says she is living with a better man than she married. More often than not, I have a positive effect when I walk into a group. Thank You, Jesus!

A final element of taming the lions is laughter. I love laughing. I like causing others to laugh. In my early years, I did that with sarcasm and verbal cut-downs. As I learned to tame the lions, I realized I didn't laugh as much and neither did those around me. It was because I got rid of the old ways I made people laugh. I started praying that Jesus would teach me how to be funny with truth in love. He did. The laughter returned, except the laughter is healthy for everyone in the room. At least, that is my goal. It is possible to be funny with truth in love, it just takes more skill than being funny with sarcasm, cut-downs, and potty humor.

Taming the tongue is vital to unity. It requires taming every thought. It can also be fun. The benefits far outweigh the training effort.

Get Interests on the Table

Another element of speaking the truth in love is getting all my interests on the table. Remember, when a group of people are trying to figure out a solution to a challenge, the **TRIPS** interests each person has are like jigsaw puzzle pieces in their pockets. People who are skilled at speaking the truth in love can easily pull their own interests out and lay them on the table.

The most effective technique I know for doing this is the "and" stance.[16] Remember all the **TRIPS** interests and

Dialectical Tensions from Chapter 4? I have many interests and they are constantly changing. What many of us do is summarize our thoughts and maybe tag on a "but" phrase that negates the first phrase. The "and" stance reminds me to accurately speak as many of my ***TRIPS*** interests as I can.

Here is how I am tempted to tell my friends about writing this book, "I am writing a book, but I can't wait to be finished with it." Here is a better description of my interests that may lead to some effective solutions.

> Every time I have prayed the last five years asking Jesus what I should do, the thought, "Finish the book." comes to mind. And I do not feel skilled enough in syntax and grammar to write an effective book. And I think I could hire professionals to help with grammar and syntax. And I researched the publishing industry and realized it takes skills I do not possess to get a book published without paying a lot of money myself. And Colette and I are willing to spend some money to publish this book. And I am not sure many people will read the book. And it doesn't matter. To be obedient to Jesus, I need to finish the book.

Please realize you can remove the "And" every time it appears as the first word of the sentence in the example above. The point is not which word you use, the point is to get as many interests out in the open as possible. When you speak or write the intangible underlying (**RIPS**) interests, you make them tangible. When they are tangible, they are much easier to resolve.

In the ideal world, the person sending the message is speaking the truth in love, and the person receiving the message is being quick to listen. If you are sending a message to an unskilled listener, you might say, "Do you mind telling me what you heard me say, so I can ensure I accurately communicated my thoughts?" I have found this question helps the other person listen well. Notice I did not say, "Please tell me what you heard me say." In the former question, I make a request and shoulder the responsibility for the communication. In the latter statement, I give a command and insinuate the other person is at fault in the communication. Most people respond better to a respectful request.

Words are like fire. We have looked at two great ways to skillfully use them. First, work hard to tame the lions. Second, speak the truth in love to get interests on the table. However, no matter how much I grow in Jesus and train, I still blow it sometimes and burn people with my thoughts and words. What then?

Chapter 11—Forgiveness

If you do not forgive others, then your Father will not forgive your transgressions – Matthew 6:15

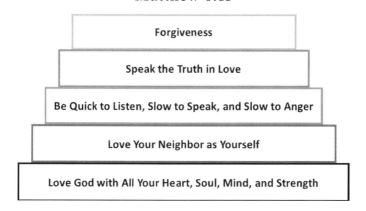

Forgiveness

Speak the Truth in Love

Be Quick to Listen, Slow to Speak, and Slow to Anger

Love Your Neighbor as Yourself

Love God with All Your Heart, Soul, Mind, and Strength

Forgiveness plays a vital role in unity. We frequently offend one another because each of us is an imperfect being. A key indicator there is an unforgiven offense is when the group keeps trying to find a solution to a problem, and one or more people keep bringing up a point we have already covered. This is a little different than people repeating themselves and getting louder with each repetition—the sign someone does not feel heard. Lack of forgiveness causes people to bring up a point we thought we solved minutes, hours, days, weeks, months, or years ago.

Forgiveness is important. A group cannot effectively finalize and implement forward-moving solutions if unforgiveness exists in the group. Thus, in the training pyramid, forgiveness comes before creative thinking.

I was teaching forgiveness to a seminary class in Malawi. One of the students raised her hand and said, "Sir, we do not do forgiveness in Africa."

I am grateful to Jesus for the reply that came to my mind and went out my mouth, "We don't do forgiveness in America either [yet another reason 80% of groups are stuck muddling along]. I am not here to teach African or American culture. We are here to learn how to live Christ's culture."

Forgiveness works miracles! Stories abound of amazing grace flooding into personal and national situations when forgiveness happens. I have walked many people through forgiveness sessions, and watched stress and years of bitterness melt away. Sometimes it melts instantly; more often, it takes weeks or months. Whatever the time frame, forgiveness is the key.

I have yet to figure out a way to prove this, but I think skilled forgiveness is a deposit of five to 10,000 in all participants' emotional bank accounts. That is incredible, considering most emotional bank account deposits are one. This means an effective ask for forgiveness is the best chance anyone has for making a negative emotional bank account balance become positive.

If you want to revitalize important relationships, and enjoy living with the people around you, then you need to be quick to ask and give forgiveness. There are two steps: learn how and do it afraid.

Learn How

The fundamentals of forgiveness are easy to learn.

Here is the illustration I use in seminars. I have a 10-foot rope with a bowling ball attached to the middle. I ask a volunteer to help me. I have the volunteer stand off to the side, then I pick up one end of the rope and quickly whip it in a circle through the air, so it makes a whistling sound.

"I used to have a bad habit." I say. Then I whip the rope through the air again.

"I used to frequently say words that wounded people." This time I whip the rope though the air and slap a chair with it, which usually makes a nice "Thwack!" sound.

"That is the affect wounding words have on a person."

Then, I turn to the volunteer and say, "Let's just imagine that chair thwack was your arm." As I wrap my end of the rope around my hand a couple of times, I have the volunteer do the same with their end of the rope.

Then I say, "Now we have an offense between us. Notice I, the offender, am attached to the weight (the bowling ball) of the offense, and the offended is attached to the weight of the offense."

Then I say, "Most people want to believe that you can ignore an offense and it will go away." As I say that, I start walking around pulling the bowling ball and the volunteer with me. Normally, the volunteer cooperates by stumbling around the stage as I tug. Sometimes, I get an aggressive volunteer who starts tugging back and makes me stumble.

Either way, the demonstration is accurate, and I say, "Notice we are still attached and our actions affect each other. Even though neither of us wants to be connected to the other, we just can't let go of the offense. I think we all have witnessed and participated in enough offenses to see the accuracy of this demonstration. I know stories of people half way around the world from each other who still get aggravated any time they think, or hear, of the other person."

The demonstration is not over. Here comes the good part. I turn to the volunteer and say, "Will you forgive me?"

As I say those words, I unwrap the rope from around my hand, then say, "Asking forgiveness is the only way to let go of the offense. Are we able to repair the relationship? No. Not until the offended forgives; however, I am free from the weight."

Then, I coach the volunteer to say, "I forgive you," then release the rope.

Finally, I say, "Now we are free of the offense and can leave it behind to move forward with the relationship."

At that point the volunteer leaves the stage, and I have the same conversation with the audience I am about to have with you.

This demonstration brings up a controversy about forgiveness: should you offer forgiveness before I ask? There are many books and articles on the subject. Two that give the general gist of the debate are by Chris Brauns[21] and Nancy Leigh DeMoss.[22] Brauns argues you should not forgive until someone asks forgiveness. DeMoss thinks it is helpful to give forgiveness regardless of whether the other asks. I find it entertaining that they both use some of the same stories as illustrations. My opinion, it depends on the situation.

The goal is to get the opportunity to rebuild the relationship. Rebuilding cannot begin until both are free from the offense. The reason not to forgive until asked? If offenders lack understanding, and think they are free of the offense the moment you give forgiveness, then they will never ask for forgiveness, and will be left holding the weight of the offense forever. Ouch! In turn, the offense will continue to hinder your relationships. However, stories abound, especially during attempts to heal from atrocities, of a person offering forgiveness and that act causing a domino effect of asking and giving forgiveness for many people, even a nation (think Desmond Tutu and South Africa Apartheid). The general rule is: forgive in your heart, so you are free of the offense, then wait to voice that forgiveness until the offender asks. Be open to Jesus overturning the general rule.

Once both parties are free of the offense, healing can begin. Part of the challenge of forgiveness is people want the relationship to go back to the way it was before the offense(s). That cannot happen. You can only move into "the new normal." Frequently, the new normal is better than the relationship was before.

Sometimes the new normal means ceasing interactions and/or creating lots of physical distance between parties until one or more parties gets healthy enough to have good relationships. Remember, this book is about functioning well together in unity; so, I am narrowing the scope of this section to offenses that do not require ceasing interactions or maintaining distance.

Wounds and loss cause grief. Grief adds layers to rebuilding. A study on grief is beyond the scope of this book. Suffice it to say there are three to seven stages of grief, depending on which research you read. Researchers agree grieving is different for each person—the stages last for different amounts of time, go in different order, and can randomly repeat. Grief is a confounding factor that makes figuring out a relationship's new normal an exercise in patience.

Now that we understand the principles of forgiveness, let's move to the really practical stuff.

Gary Chapman and Jennifer Thomas did some wonderful work on forgiveness.[23] Their basic premise is there are five elements.

1. Admit.
2. Express regret.
3. Offer restitution.
4. Repent.
5. Ask forgiveness.

Or, as my wife likes to remember the list.

1. I did it.
2. I'm sorry.
3. How can I make it up to you?
4. Here is how I'm changing.
5. Will you forgive me?

Most people in the world prefer one or two of the elements over the others; so, if you prefer I "admit," yet I only "repent," you probably will not forgive me. Given how hard it is to figure out someone's language of apology, the smart move is to hit all five elements every time you ask forgiveness. Let me illustrate.

At a former job, I was standing outside my general manager's (GM) office one day when someone told him a new kid just drove forklift forks through a garage door. My GM got mad and started shouting. The most interesting thing he said was, "Well, is he crying!?" Maybe that was insight that the GM's language of apology is "express regret." The new kid never told the GM. He just slinked around trying to avoid the GM. They did not have a good relationship from that day forward.

A few weeks later, I was driving a forklift. I didn't see a pallet sticking out on the second shelf, drove into it, and broke a light on the forklift. My adrenaline kicked in, and I felt my heart pounding, until I took a deep breath and reminded myself, "I know how to ask forgiveness." As I was walking toward his office with the light fragments in my hand I rehearsed the five elements of forgiveness, then thought, "This will be a good test to see if forgiveness works." I knocked on his door, then asked, "Is this a convenient moment to talk?"

He waved me in.

I said, "I broke this forklift light by running into a pallet that was sticking out (admit). I'm sorry (express regret). I don't know the company policy on stuff like this, and I'm willing to pay to replace the light (offer restitution). I'm willing to take extra training or whatever. I thought I was

94

already being careful, but I assure you I will redouble my care after this (repent—plan for change). Is there anything else I need to do to make this right (ask forgiveness)?"

He smiled and said, "You don't need to pay for it. Accidents happen. We're good."

There may be other factors in the difference between his two reactions. I am convinced the biggest factor was I asked forgiveness well, and the kid did not.

Notice in the forgiveness step, I did not say, "Will you forgive me?" For some reason, that question is awkward in most professional environments. Here are some phrases that suffice for that step in those situations.

1. Are we good to go?
2. What else do I need to do to make this right?
3. What else do I need to do to keep us moving forward?

Chapman's simple model is good for little offenses and accidents. What about the long-term effects of our addictions and other bad habits? Under the directions of Sharon Bayus, Innovative Alternatives, Inc. (IA) developed a model (Appendix B)[24] that I, and others, have used with great success to find freedom and better relationships. When IA gave me permission to include their model in this book, Sharon wrote:

The reason forgiveness is often incomplete, is because we only say we are sorry for the injurious behavior (frequently followed by an excuse for that behavior), and we never address the impact of our actions on the other person, making it very difficult for them not to hold it over our heads in the future. I really think that is the primary revelation the Lord gave me when He dropped this process in my mind.

I agree. Almost every time I walk people through this model, the most challenging thing to get them to do is refrain from adding "but if you . . ." after admitting what they did. In other words, instead of saying, "I am sorry I lied." Most people will say, "I am sorry I lied, but if you hadn't been so angry . . ." We will discuss why we so powerfully feel the need to point out other people's faults and minimize our own.

In the meantime, here is another painful, yet hopeful, story from my past.

As Sharon Bayus was teaching this model during our reconciliation training, I felt convicted. I went home that night, sat down with my wife, and asked her if I could ask forgiveness for all the years of fits of anger and harsh words. I further asked if I could keep IA's model in front of me, and use it as a cheat sheet because I was not yet skilled with it. My wife, gracious as ever, agreed.

"Colette, I have thrown fits of anger like a two-year old for years. When I throw them, I wound you with words and attitudes."

At this point, I listed the worst incidents, then asked if I needed to add more. When she was satisfied all the required memories were on the list, I continued.

"Saying, 'I'm sorry' seems insufficient. How can I just say, 'I'm sorry' for belittling you, humiliating you, watching our children's eyes and countenance drop as they slink away . . ." I think you get the point. I listed out all the ways I could think of that my fits affected her and the girls.

Then, I did the hardest part of the IA model. I asked, "What other ways did my fits affect you that I have not mentioned?"

At that point, Colette gave me permission to put the listening model (Appendix A) in front of me. She courageously listed a few damaging effects of my fits that I had not realized. I expressed regret for each of those too.

I combined the restitution and repentance elements by saying, "If I had stolen money from you, I could pay you back plus 20%. I cannot think of a way to pay you back for damaging words, actions, and reactions (Relax, I never physically abused my wife. Verbal, and non-verbal, fits are bad enough). The only thing I have to offer as restitution is my repentance (plan for change). The challenging thing about my plan for change is we both know the reality of trying to change generational junk (sin tendencies passed down through nature, nurture, and personal choices). We both know I cannot promise you I will never throw a fit again. All I can offer is:

1. I am memorizing scripture about controlling the tongue and staying calm.
2. I will tell the other instructors at DM that I struggle with this, and ask them to hold me accountable.
3. I am determined to make every thought in my mind, and word from my mouth, give grace to those who hear.

I went on, "And I realize that is easy for me to say. You and the children are the ones who bear the brunt of my relapses. If you want me to move away until I can control myself, I will do so. Is there something else you can think of that will protect you and the girls until I am healthy?"

Colette thought for a few moments. She said that she appreciated my thoughts, did not think I needed to go away, and agreed my training plan was the best option we had.

I continued, "Then what I am asking you to do is stay in relationship with me knowing that I will probably wound you again. Knowing the only thing I can offer you is a determination that it will be longer until the next fit happens, the fit will have less intensity, and I will immediately pull both these models out and do this forgiveness process again."

If memory serves me correctly, I was crying at that point, just like I am crying right now typing this story.

Then I asked, "Will you forgive me and continue to live with me?"

I slid the IA model to Colette. My amazing wife read the forgiveness response, sat back, took a deep breath, looked me in the eye and said, "I forgive you for. . . ." She listed off every incident and summary I had listed.

She continued, "I appreciate you asking forgiveness, and I am willing to risk rebuilding trust and going through this process as many times as it takes to help break this generational junk."

We didn't keep track of the number of times we had to go through this process together. Each time she said she was willing to continue because *every* time the amount of time between "asks" was longer, and the fit was less intense than ever before.

As of this typing, I don't think I have thrown a fit worthy of the IA model for at least four years. I have thrown small ones worthy of the Chapman quick model, but even those are getting few and far between.

Praise Jesus! Forgiveness works to rebuild relationships. It works on small wounds, large wounds, long-term addictions, and generational bad habits. It even works if the offender needs to be out of the scene for a while to become healthy.

Do It Afraid

In adrenaline sports, the adrenaline does not subside until you start the activity. Forgiveness is like an adrenaline sport. Usually you must ask forgiveness while you are feeling afraid. The nervous/embarrassed feelings usually do not go away until you are well into the forgiveness process. That is OK. Do it afraid! Do it regardless of what your emotions try to get you to do or not do.

Do you need a little more proof that you should be asking and giving forgiveness? Look at these two excerpts from the Sermon on the Mount.

> Therefore, if you are presenting your offering at the altar, and there remember that your brother has something against you, leave your offering there before the altar and go; first be reconciled to your brother, and then come and present your offering. Matthew 5:23-24.

> For if you forgive others for their transgressions, your heavenly Father will also forgive you. But if

100

you do not forgive others, then your Father will

not forgive your transgressions. Matthew 6:14-15.

There it is, from the mouth of Jesus, in one of the most important sermons He preached. The moment you realize you offended someone, you are to go ask forgiveness. When someone asks forgiveness, you need to forgive.

Why are we so scared to ask forgiveness? In North American cultures I think the main reason is fear of the future. We don't understand the difference between contribution and fault[9]. Let me explain.

When something goes wrong, our instant reaction is to try to find who was at fault. There is a good reason people want to assign fault. Fault implies that you did everything wrong and I did everything right. If I can prove it was your fault, then I bear little or no responsibility to change or make effort toward a solution. Fault is focused on retribution for the past. Most often, if people determine I am at fault, I suffer in some way.

A more scriptural view is figuring out and fixing contribution. Let's go back to the Sermon on the Mount.

Why do you look at the speck that is in your

brother's eye, but do not notice the log that is in

your own eye? Or how can you say to your

brother, 'Let me take the speck out of your eye,'

and behold, the log is in your own eye? You hypocrite, first take the log out of your own eye, and then you will see clearly to take the speck out of your brother's eye. Matthew 7:3-5.

Contribution focuses on what I did to contribute to this mess. It also aims at what I can do to help clean up this mess and fix our future interactions. Life is rarely as simple as fault implies. Usually, all parties involved, including the Systemic Expectations (remember, the **S** in *TRIPS*), contribute in one way or another to the challenge the group faces. A huge attitude that helps resolve disagreements more quickly and more effectively is for all parties involved to be on the lookout for their contributions, and for the group to figure out ways to fix all contributions so they don't happen in the future. Instead of pointing fingers to determine punishment, it is *much* more helpful to rub chins to figure out how to fix the future.

Most of us think, "People will assign me fault if I ask forgiveness. It was not my fault! It was their fault!"

Yes. Most of us are skilled at seeing other people's contributions while, at the same time, ignoring our own. Someone has to risk opening honest dialog by asking forgiveness. Most of the time, one person admitting contribution and asking forgiveness frees others in the group to do the same.

Scripture tells us to do many things that are risky in our culture. Asking forgiveness is just one of Jesus' commands that really tests whether you believe He will provide for your future if you risk following Him.

You *can* substantially lower the risk by skillfully asking forgiveness for contribution.

At one point in our family, we all agreed Kiersten, one of my four daughters, was responsible to do the laundry. We drew lines on the insides of the laundry baskets and she agreed she needed to keep the laundry below those lines. Everyone else in the family was responsible to take their laundry to the main laundry baskets. One day I came home, and three of the laundry baskets had laundry above the line. The next day I came home, and three of the laundry baskets had laundry above the line. That evening we got in the car for a trip to visit Grandma and Grandpa. On the way, I told Kiersten I had seen the laundry baskets full for two days. I then launched into a tirade about fulfilling responsibilities, how important chores are to family health, and went on and on . . . and on . . . and on. Finally, I saw Colette's that-is-quite-enough look. I realized that I just broke many of the principles in this book. Kiersten was crying. The other girls were trying to disappear in their seats. Colette had a here-we-go-again look on her face.

I was rationalizing in my head. I am the father! I am responsible to train my children to work hard and fulfill their responsibilities in this world. I am not going to back down from this because that will weaken the authority of the father in this house and lead to all sorts of chaos in the future.

Then I breathed in through my nose, out through my mouth, quoted a few reminder scriptures in my mind, relaxed, and realized I needed to ask forgiveness for my contributions in order to get us back on track. I took a few more deep breaths as I reviewed the Chapman forgiveness model. Then the miracle began.

"OK, I blew it again," I said. "Yes, I am the father. I am responsible to God for training my children (I find listing my responsibilities is a good foundation for contribution rather than fault); however, I know that long tirades are not training, they are fits. I know that correcting a person publicly is humiliation, not training. I also know that jumping to conclusions before learning the whole story only contributes to the problem and hinders finding solutions. I also know doing all this on the way to Grandma and Grandpa's ruins the trip (admit). I am sorry for doing each of those things the past 20 minutes (express regret). I will do all the laundry from all the baskets in the house when we get home to give us a good jump start on whatever solution we are about to figure out (restitution). I hope I have not had a tirade like this for a long time. I am training hard to get to the point where I never go on tirades (repent). Will you forgive me (the ask)?"

Everyone in the car was honest at that point. Colette voiced her forgiveness. The girls said they needed to recover a bit first.

On the way home that evening, the girls voiced their forgiveness. Then we all discussed what had happened with the laundry. Both days, Kiersten had come through in the morning and done the laundry to get the baskets below the lines. The other girls had both saved up their laundry for over a week in their rooms. The first day, Devin brought Mount Laundry from her room and dumped it in the family baskets right before I arrived home. The second day, Brenyn brought Mount Laundry from her room and dumped it into the family baskets right before I got home. Everyone did the Systemic Expectations we instituted; however, our expectations were flawed.

During our dialog on the way home, we realized we all needed to take our laundry to the family baskets every morning before Kiersten did the morning laundry. At the end of this discussion the girls asked Kiersten's forgiveness for putting her in that bind. Kiersten asked forgiveness from all of us for getting frustrated about the plan; yet, not mentioning her frustration. We all forgave each other. When we arrived home, we all went cheerfully in the house. Laundry functioned well for a few months until the next time one of us got frustrated with the plan, and we had to re-visit the laundry plan.

Life is challenging. We are all pursuing multiple levels of constantly changing interests. Plans fall apart because the goals underlying them change. We usually don't realize we have changed until we start offending each other. Even when life is chugging along as we anticipated, we still accidently wound each other because we are far from perfect. The reason forgiveness is the fifth building block of the training pyramid is that it is easier to do if you are calm, have high emotional bank accounts, and are skilled at listening and speaking truth in love. Why is forgiveness foundational to creative thinking? If an unforgiven offense exists in the group, it will constantly be lurking under the surface making all attempts at creative thinking more challenging. Perhaps the grace and compassion we show each other during forgiveness re-charges our creative nature as God's image bearers. Forgiveness is potent and vital. Please do it.

Chapter 12—Creative Thinking

In the beginning God created the heavens and the earth. – Genesis 1:1

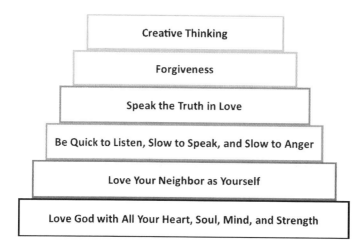

Creative thinking is vital for unity. What other way are we going to craft solutions that meet all our *TRIPS* goals? If you do not remember what *TRIPS* goals are, you might re-read Chapter 2. Do you want:

1. Vacations every family member enjoys?
2. Family members to do household chores without being told, maybe even cheerfully?
3. Frustrations at work and church to morph into satisfying solutions?

Then, think creatively.

I would rather get teeth pulled than go to Disney World.

I had a training trip in southern Florida. Colette and I decided to take extra days on either end and turn it into a family vacation. When the girls (our children are all female) heard the plan, they instantly started talking about Disney World. Tension began to build in our home until we decided to set a couple of hours aside to practice the principles in this book.

How can we all enjoy a vacation to Florida? We each took turns talking about our experiences with vacations. While one person spoke, the rest of us tried to stay fully present and actively listen. We set up a projector screen and connected it to a computer so we could visibly list each person's *TRIPS* goals.

Some painful stories from past vacations surfaced. We asked for, and gave, forgiveness as needed.

When we finished that session, we had a list of interesting goals. Here is the summary of that list.

1. Colette and the girls wanted to experience as many new activities and fun places as possible.

2. I wanted to relax and take off my watch—nowhere to be and nothing to do.

3. We all wanted to enjoy being around each other during the entire trip.

How could we possibly be together, and all have a vacation we would relish? Will the Freeman family languish in mediocre-vacation land forever?

I am using this shameless cliff-hanger technique to motivate you to read through the following tips and tricks.

There are many great books, websites, seminars, and other trainings for creative thinking. Here are five I have found useful:

1. Fredrik Haren's <u>The Idea Book</u>.[25]
2. Michael Michalko's <u>Thinkertoys</u>.[26]
3. Kevin and Shawn Coynes' <u>Brainsteering</u>.[27]
4. Gordon Smith's <u>The Voice of Jesus</u>[28] has a chapter on communal discernment that helps a group discern Jesus' directions.
5. Mindtools.com has an excellent problem-solving section.

It is a lifetime pursuit to know which creative thinking process to use and how to use it. Here are three determining factors:

1. What question(s) do you want to answer? You need a different process for figuring out who will do which household chores than you do for figuring out what Jesus' vision is for your ministry.
2. How many people need to be involved? Five people need a different creative thinking process than 20

people, and 20 people need a much different process than 500 people.

3. How much time, money, emotional bank account, and other resources do you have? It is a much different process with a million dollars, ten weeks, and healthy relationships than with one hundred dollars, one hour, and two people in conflict.

Back to our vacation challenge.

After we asked for and received forgiveness, we were able to address the Disney World option with truth in love. We all want to go to Disney World; however, we only have enough money to go for one day. I do not want the personal challenge of trying to stay happy while we run ourselves ragged trying to get our money's worth. When we go to Disney World, I want to be able to go for a few relaxed days. After my logical presentation, Colette and the girls still wanted to go for a day. I was desperate, so I said, "What if I paid for each of you to do some really cool thing on this trip that you have always wanted to do? Would you be willing to do that instead of go to Disney World?" Every female in the room lit up with a large smile and sparkling eyes.

I inadvertently took their minds back to one of their main goals for the trip—experiencing new activities and fun places. I helped them realize Disney World was the first thing that popped into their head; however, it was not the only option. Possibly, it was not the best option.

What most of us naturally do when we face a challenge is quickly come up with a plan, fixate on that plan, then fight for that plan as if the world will fall apart if the group does not enact that plan. For better solutions, we need to look at all the interests we have put on the table and try to fit them together in the best way.

Creative thinking is anything you do to get yourself out of that fixation mode to come up with other viable plans. Why does it help to do creative thinking with a group? Each person has limited perspectives on the challenge. The more perspectives you get, the better plan you can create.

Yes, it takes more effort to create a plan together than it does to create it alone. Keep reading, we will discuss in the next section of the book how to determine if the challenge is worth the effort of involving more people.

In our case, we agreed that to craft a thorough vacation plan, we needed to come up with as many answers to the following questions as possible.

1. What new experiences do I want to have?
2. How do I want to relax?
3. How can we enjoy being together?
4. How do we pay for this trip?

(Are you thinking creatively enough to realize this list of questions could easily be tweaked to relate to what new product a business wants to launch or ministry a church wants to start? Creative thinking processes help in every arena, not just family vacations.)

We decided to re-convene in a week after we had a chance to research, and mull over, options.

The next week we generated a couple pages of possible answers to our questions. After that session, we took another week-long break so we could think about the options and our goals. We had several fun conversations through that week, many of them around the breakfast table, as each of us thought of all the combinations of possibilities.

A week later we took the next step in the unity process.

Chapter 13—Decide

. . . choose for yourselves today . . .

– Joshua 24:15 ripped out of context

Decide

Creative Thinking

Forgiveness

Speak the Truth in Love

Be Quick to Listen, Slow to Speak, and Slow to Anger

Love Your Neighbor as Yourself

Love God with All Your Heart, Soul, Mind, and Strength

Your group has an extensive list of creative answers to the question(s). How do you pick the one(s) you are going to use? Many of the solutions will work; however, *we* can only enact one of them at a time. How do you pick *the* one?

Remember **TRIPS** from Chapter 2? This is the Process (**P**) level of disagreements.

There are two major challenges with decisions. First, there are several decision-making processes. Each process builds unity if used in the right circumstances. Each process weakens unity if used in the wrong circumstances. Kenneth

Thomas and Ralph Kilmann's research shows that, without training, most people use one conflict style (a.k.a. decision-making process) for all situations.[5] For a group to function with unity, it needs to choose and use the best decision-making process for each situation. Group members often disagree which process they should use.

Second, once the group chooses a process, every member in the group needs to effectively fulfill his or her role in that decision-making process. Have you ever watched a basketball coach stand up and give a hand signal, then watch the players on the court instantly switch from man-to-man defense to zone defense? That is an incredible teamwork switch that takes hours of practice to perfect because all players must understand the overall structure of each defense and their roles within the structure. If one player on the team stays in man-to-man mindset after everyone else switches to zone, the teamwork falls apart. It is the same in every meeting between two or more people. If the people involved use different processes, and/or are not effectively fulfilling their roles within the processes, the unity falls apart.

There is hope! It is possible for a team to become skilled at using appropriate processes for different challenges. Grasping the reality of the few paragraphs you just read in this chapter is a *huge* step forward. Next, you need to learn the different options and how to choose.

Each group must figure out systems that work best for them; however, studying decision tools others use, may provide shortcuts in the process. I hope you grasp the following concepts enough to design a model that works for your group. Until then, here is my attempt to blend the Vroom-Yetton-Jago Decision Model[29] logic, the Thomas-Kilmann Conflict Model,[5] and the principles from this book to help your team choose the best process for individuals, and the group, to use for different circumstances.

Disagreement Processes for Individuals

According to Thomas and Kilmann, there are five basic conflict styles individuals use. Most of us are stuck in a rut of using one mode for every situation, which is like a carpenter only using a hammer to construct a house. A person skilled in disagreements chooses the appropriate style for the circumstance.

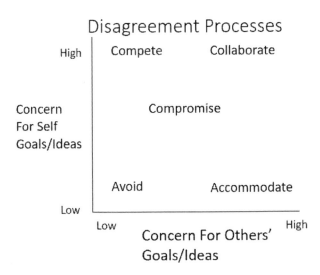

Disagreement Processes

As the chart shows, there are five disagreement processes. To illustrate, let's look at the story of two girls who want the same orange. We'll also look at pros and cons of each process.

1. Avoid—If both girls are avoiders they will talk about the weather, boys, or math class without ever mentioning the orange. Obviously, neither girl gets what she wants.

    Avoiding is appropriate when the task is not vital, and the long-term health of the relationship does not matter. For instance, if you are standing in a grocery store and see a mother holding a child who is screaming for candy, you probably should not get involved in that disagreement.

Avoiding is inappropriate when the task and long-term health of the relationship are important. Avoiding is a withdrawal from the Emotional Bank Accounts[14] of those around you. It also follows a classic pattern of avoid, avoid, Avoid, *Blow!* There is a reason "blow" describes an avoider and a volcano. When an avoider blows, relationships suffer damage.

2. Accommodate—If both girls are accommodators, they will probably have a polite fight, "Here, you take the orange." "Oh, no, I couldn't possibly. You take the orange." "Please, I insist. You take the orange." This might go on until they decide to donate the orange to charity. Again, neither girl gets what she wants.

Accommodating is appropriate when the task is vital, the long-term health of the relationship does not matter, or I want to make some emotional bank account deposits into another person and can temporarily do so. This is the style privates in the army use during a battle—they just do what they are

117

told. Perhaps employees should use it when the owner of the company arrives to inspect their division. I sometimes use it to build emotional bank account with another person when I know I need to have a challenging conversation with a person and need to build some cushion first.

Accommodating is inappropriate when the long-term health of the relationship matters. You see the accommodating pattern frequently in churches—also, in homes where children have no chores and parents do all the work. A person frequently accommodates, then tells as many people as will listen, "No one knows or appreciates what I do around here. It doesn't bother me, mind you, because Christ calls us to serve, but it would be nice to hear, 'Thanks!' occasionally." People quickly tire of hearing those complaints. Accommodators may not realize it, but their emotional bank accounts get depleted every time they accommodate, which means they eventually do not want to be around the people they are serving.

3. Compromise—If both girls are compromisers, the orange challenge is quick and easy. "Hey, there is an

orange. How about I cut it in two and you choose which side you want?" The other girl says, "OK." Seems like a good solution, however, neither girl got what she wants.

Compromising is appropriate when the task is not vital, you don't want to use time on the decision, and you have enough positive emotional bank account with the other to make some withdrawal. I learned the tactic in this illustration because my sister-in-law successfully used it with her two boys to split desserts.

Compromise is not appropriate when the task and the long-term health of the relationship are important. Look at government politics to see what compromise does long-term.

4. Compete—If both girls compete they might try to snatch the orange first, have an eloquent debate or shouting match (depending on their debate skill), or it might even break into a fist fight.

    Competing is appropriate when the task is more vital than the temporary health of the relationship.

For instance, when I was a child standing at the edge of a road waiting to cross, I looked one-way then started running across. Mid-stride, I felt my dad grab me by the shirt and yank me back. I looked at my dad and saw a stern look. I got mad. He did not consider that his action might make me mad. He only wanted to keep the car, that he saw and I did not, from squishing me.

Competing is inappropriate for extended use when the long-term health of the relationship is vital. The winner causes a *huge* emotional bank account withdrawal with the loser. When one person loses, the relationship loses. My emotional bank account with my dad could afford that rare protective yank; however, if my dad had made a habit of directing me by yanking my shirt, our relationship would have quickly soured.

5. Collaborate—If both girls are collaborators, they would discuss why each one wants the orange. They would find out one is hungry and knows a whole orange is the perfect amount of food for her. The other is headed for science class and needs a complete orange peel for a lab. Ah, a simple

solution. The one who needs the whole orange peel thoroughly washes her hands, carefully peels the orange, and leaves the fruit for her friend.

Collaboration is appropriate when the task is vital, and we have plenty of time. It builds emotional bank account for all involved. It is the mode that best meets Philippians 2:4—"do not merely look out for your own personal interests, but also for the interests of others."

Collaboration is inappropriate when time is limited, which is why few people use it. Most of us run around at a frantic pace thinking we have little time. It is easy to talk and write about these five styles. The challenge is getting skilled enough to use the style that is best for the moment, rather than using our preferred style in every situation.

Decision Processes for Groups

Now let's talk about the five decision processes at the group level. Maybe I'll change my mind someday, but at this point, I don't think Avoid and Accommodate apply at the group level. Like all five styles, they can be appropriate choices for individuals during group decisions. They just do not apply to an overall group decision making structure.

Group decision processes are on a continuum. On one end is Compete. On the other end is Collaborate. Compromise, of course, is appropriate somewhere in between. If you want to figure out ten or twenty options for your group to choose from, have at it. My experience is a group is doing well to get skilled at using the following four: Intensive Care (IC), Leader Invites Private Input, Leader Invites Public Input, or Collaborate.

Intensive Care (IC)

The leader makes the decision and informs the group of the decision after the fact. Even if the leader is trying to consider the goals and ideas of others, the leader is using Compete. After they are informed, group members need to go along with the decision as if it was their own decision. If a group member is struggling to do so, the member needs to make an appointment with the leader to dialog to figure out if:

1. The group needs to use a different process and revisit the decision.
2. The leader needs to be more careful about using this process in the future.
3. The group member needs to mature in some way.

4. Or a combination of these options.

That is a challenging dialog which requires both people to be proficient in all the Chapter 2 skills. I never said unity is easy, just possible.

The extreme example of this process is Incident Command, which is the process the military, police, and medical groups use during an emergency. The leader makes the calls. Everyone else accommodates. Forgiveness and dialogs about improvements in group processes wait until the emergency is finished. The Discovery Ministries team had to be proficient in this mode in case of a lost camper or medical emergency.

One of the peak moments of my career occurred during the Joplin, Missouri, tornado response in 2011. A new person in the team said, "I keep hearing the initials 'IC.' What does that stand for?" One of the team leaders said, "It stands for Incident Command." Another team leader responded, "No it doesn't. It stands for Intensive Care because that is what the Discovery Ministries team has done for us the last four days!" That moment was huge confirmation for me that the principles in this book are effective.

Leader Invites Private Input

The leader informs the group, "We need to make this decision by (whatever deadline). I think the decision is simple enough I can just make it. If you want me to consider your thoughts on the matter before making the decision, please talk with me ASAP." At the appointed time, the leader makes the decision, then informs the group. The leader is mildly competing and offering to collaborate, compromise, or mildly compete with members. Each group member has the option to accommodate, compromise, collaborate, or compete. If a member chooses to avoid, that person is committing to support the leader's decision wholeheartedly. If a member has strong concerns about the decision, that member is responsible to communicate the truth in love with the leader ASAP.

Leader Invites Public Input

The leader gathers the group members and tells them, "I plan to make this decision after we have talked unless you convince me that we need to follow a different decision process." The leader facilitates the discussion. Again, the leader is mildly competing, and offering to compromise, collaborate, or mildly compete with members. Every member should stay fully present in the dialog using accommodate, compromise, collaborate, or compete. After the decision is made, every team member should wholeheartedly support it.

Collaborate

The leader initiates collaboration by handing the process over to the facilitator. Every group member needs to stay fully present and collaborate during the process. There are many ways for a group to effectively collaborate. You must have an effective facilitator—a person highly skilled in all the principles in Chapter 2—who is willing and able to champion a healthy solution finding process while staying neutral about the solution.

It also takes a highly skilled group to have the leader in the room and still collaborate. It is an even rarer group in which the leader can function as the facilitator. It is hard for the leader to be neutral about the decision, and harder for group members to perceive that the leader is neutral about the decision.

For a group to function with unity, it *must* frequently use collaboration. However, even collaboration can become a rut when we use it to make non-vital decisions, and/or time is of the essence. I never said this is easy; however, it is worth the effort.

Now you know at least four basic group styles. How does the leader determine which decision process to use? I use three basic questions as a filter.

1. How vital is the task?
2. How much time do we have?
3. How are the emotional bank account levels between group members (a.k.a. esprit de corps)?

At one end of the spectrum is Intensive Care (IC). Use this process when the answers to the first two questions are, (1) the task is vital and (2) you have precious little time because it is an emergency. During an emergency, you don't even consider the third question. Just realize, emotional bank accounts and relationships get damaged during intensive care, even when it is done with love and respect. A wise team works hard to build esprit de corps (healthy relationships) during normal times, so the group can stay healthy during and after an emergency. The leader also initiates forgiveness sessions after the event to help heal the interpersonal wounds.

Leader Invites Private Input works when (1) the task is not vital, (2) we don't want to use much time on the decision, and (3) the leader has high enough emotional bank accounts with group members to risk a withdrawal from each member. The amount of emotional bank account withdrawal is different for each group member based on how much the member trusts the leader and many other factors.

Leader Invites Public Input is, obviously, a little further down the continuum. (1) The task may or may not be more vital than Leader Invites Private Input, (2) we don't mind using more time, and (3) we are less willing to risk emotional bank account loss with the leader. You are verging on needing to collaborate, but don't want to use that much time.

At the other end of the spectrum is Collaborate. Do this when (1) the task is vital, (2) we have ample time, and (3) we want to make deposits in group members' emotional bank accounts. Please note, any group member who thinks we are collaborating unnecessarily is having an emotional bank account withdrawal during the collaboration. We will talk about the solution to this challenge in the Effective Meeting section.

Let's discuss who determines which mode a team will use. It is easiest for the leader to decide. The wise leader does a quick check to see if everyone is willing to wholeheartedly follow that style for this decision. If there is disagreement about which style to use, the leader should use the filters to determine which style is most effective. That might sound stupid, but remember, the *P* (Process) is part of the (*RIPS*) that will cause all sorts of challenges if unresolved.

Who is the leader? On a skilled team, the person in charge of an area is the leader for decisions affecting that area. For instance, if the director of a camp walks into the camp kitchen, the director needs to realize that in the kitchen, the head cook is the leader and the director is a team member. A wise director will only step in to become the leader in the kitchen if the head cook is floundering as leader. If the cook disagrees with the director taking over, the director's emotional bank account with the head cook will plummet.

Whew! We are finished conceptualizing the different decision processes for the individuals and the group. Perhaps this chart will help bring together the Individual Disagreement Processes and the Group Decision Processes.

		Appropriate Individual Disagreement Process Given Group Position				
		Compete	Collaborate	Compromise	Avoid	Accommodate
Group Decision Process	*Intensive Care*	Leader				Member
	Leader Invites Private Input	Mildly - Members and Leader	Members	Members	Members	Members
	Leader Invites Public Input	Mildly - Members and Leader	Members	Members		Members
	Collaborate		Facilitator, members			

Now, you and your team need to train. We will discuss training more in Part III. Practically, I think it is wise to admit to yourselves which decision style rut you are in. Then, clarify each person's role for that rut; so, at least you can skillfully, rather than sloppily, do that decision process. Then get skilled at one more style and develop a signal for switching between the two. When the group is satisfied they can skillfully use both styles at will, add a third style, and so on. Effective decision making takes practice.

One of my favorite stories about a group switching modes involves a drill sergeant and his wife. Colette and I met them in our early years of marriage when we worked outside Fort Leonard Wood, Missouri, an army training base. We admired their marriage; especially because they were a military family and we knew military, and other incident command organizations, have high marital conflict and divorce rates. We asked them to tell us some of their beliefs about marriage, and he told us this story. "You have to understand, as a drill sergeant, my hat is the symbol of my authority. You could almost say the hat is the drill sergeant. I would have soldiers cover my hat with their bodies when it rained and punish them if my hat got wet. One day, I came home, walked in the door, and didn't act very nice to my wife. She grabbed my hat off my head, threw it out the door into the muddy yard, and said, 'That hat will never come in this house again.' And it hasn't. To this day, there is a hook outside our front door on which I hang my hat before I walk in the door."

We can all learn from my drill sergeant friend—choose the best decision-making process for the situation. Group members do not thrive under a leader who constantly competes.

Meanwhile, back to my family crafting a vacation every person would enjoy. We used collaboration because (1) it was vital to us that each family member be passionate about the vacation, (2) we allowed plenty of time for the decisions, and (3) one of our main goals for the whole vacation was to build emotional bank accounts between all of us. Here is what we decided.

We went to a city no one had been to before that had the activities the girls wanted to do and got a hotel room on the beach. Colette and I walked the beach at sunrise while the girls slept. We woke the girls and ate breakfast together. Then Colette and the girls explored the city while I read a book. They came back at lunch time and we ate lunch together. Then we went to mark an item off each of our bucket lists: two of the girls swam with dolphins; Colette and I took a helicopter ride with our third daughter. That evening we ate pizza in the hotel room while we watched the Olympics.

The next day we drove to my training city. Colette and the girls dropped me off at the training every morning. While they explored the city, visited museums, and otherwise crammed as much fun into the day as possible, I sat in class. They picked me up at the end of the day, and we all returned exhausted to the hotel to plop down and enjoy watching the Olympics together. We repeated that for the five days of my training.

Then, we loaded up and went to another city on a beach that none of us had ever visited. This was my three-day recuperation phase of the vacation. Each day looked the same. Colette and I woke early every morning to walk the beach. Then we woke the girls and had breakfast, after which Colette and the girls packed up to explore the city and surrounding area. I read and wrote for a while, went for a run on the beach, read and wrote some more (I have as much fun exploring new ideas as Colette and the girls do exploring the physical world), then napped. Mid-afternoon, about the time I got restless, Colette and the girls returned and took me to do the one thing they found that day that they all wanted to see or do again. While we did it I told them some of the exciting ideas I explored that morning. Each evening, we returned to the hotel room to eat some fun food (with some nutritious food thrown in) and watched the Olympics until bed time.

I neglected to mention one of the goals the girls had—to watch The Lord of the Rings movies. For months Colette and I had told them they couldn't watch the movies until they read the books (We'll do almost anything to get the girls to enjoy reading). The girls decided they wanted to finish the books on this trip, then have a movie marathon in the car to make the road trip home more enjoyable. That was a memorable idea. Reading the final book pleasantly occupied us on the road trip to Florida, and watching the movies pleasantly occupied us on the road trip home.

We had a budget. Every evening we recorded how much we spent and how much we had left. That made it possible for everyone to know what we had left, what we were spending it on, and that everything they wanted in the budget would still get done. It also did away with my family constantly doing the thing that makes a vacation miserable for me—looking at me with pleading eyes trying to get me to decide to spend money to do whatever had just popped into their heads.

We also made preparing for the trip fun. We planned nights with fun music for one, or more, of us to prepare and freeze food for the trip because carrying food we enjoy would not only be more fun, it would also give us more flexibility and better nutrition on the trip.

We also freed Colette to spend hours researching all the possible places and experiences in Florida because that research is part of the exploration fun for her, even if we don't get to do half of what she discovers. An interesting element of Colette's trip research is she just wants to do the research. She does not want to decide which of the things we do because choosing from all the possibilities feels too much like choosing one child over another. It was a breakthrough when we had a calm dialog to figure out this interesting piece of the fun-vacation puzzle.

At the end of that Florida vacation, every family member agreed it was the best vacation ever! Interestingly, we thought our collaborative pre-trip efforts built emotional bank accounts between all of us just as much as the actual trip.

It is possible for every family member to enjoy a vacation. It is possible for a group of people to make decisions in such a way that they move forward with unity.

Chapter 14—Accountability

But prove yourselves doers of the word, and not merely hearers who delude themselves.

– James 1:22

If everyone walks away from a decision thinking somebody else will do the work, there is a high likelihood no one will do the work. A decision without accountability is just good intentions; it is like rainless dark clouds during a drought—useless and disappointing. There are three vital elements for accountability: answer five accountability questions, take notes, and put the notes in a remembering system.

First answer the five accountability questions:

1. What work needs to be done?
2. Who is going to do the work?
3. When does it need to be finished?
4. What resources may be used to do the work?
5. How will we know it is finished, if more resources are needed, or if we need to call it a failure and re-group?

Second, take notes. I learned this principle from a speaker at the Governor's Leadership Forum in Missouri when I was in college. The governor brought in successful people from many fields. Most spoke for at least 30 minutes about what he or she believed made a person successful. I only remember one person's presentation. He stood up and said, "Take notes. Few people remember what was said or decided in a meeting. If you take notes, you will remember. If you remember, you will be put in charge." Then he sat down. He spoke truth.

Third, put the notes in your remembering system. You can use a calendar, agendas and minutes, a project management system, a combination of those things, or whatever else you dream up that works. Please, please, please, do not trust your brain(s) to remember, because you(they) won't. Test me on this. Wait one week after a group makes a decision. Have each member of the group write down all they can remember about that decision—without consulting any of their notes. Compare their answers. They will not match. You will get close to the same results if you wait just one hour after the decision is made.

I now think the most important contribution I make in meetings (besides making sure everyone feels heard and respected) is to make sure accountability is in place for every decision. My favorite story of the effect this has for a group is when I attended a cave rescue training. The National Cave Rescue Commission (NCRC) conducted training. The first day was lectures. The second day was a full-blown simulation. The NCRC had a government agency host the event, and opened the event to local ambulance crews and caving enthusiasts, because those are the people who typically respond to cave rescues. The morning of the simulation, NCRC divided us into ten groups. Some groups had complete ambulance crews and cavers. Some groups had government employees. Some groups just had cavers. They told us where the cave was, then randomly chose groups at 15-minute intervals and sent them to the cave. Their goal was to simulate the way rescuers arrive at a scene. I was in the ninth group sent to the cave. Their call-out plan worked—when my group arrived, everything was in chaos. I

136

was with a couple other wilderness facilitators who had wilderness medical incident command training. We evaluated the scene and decided the best thing we could do was help the poor government guy with a wild look in his eyes who was in the middle of it all barking orders (We'll call him Bob). I took out my notebook and pencil (I don't leave home without them), walked up beside Bob, and started writing down his orders. Three minutes later, he said, "Hey, where is John!?" I calmly said, "You sent John to the mouth of the cave two minutes ago to get you a walkie talkie." (Why did I know that? Because I wrote it down two minutes ago and could quickly look it up.) Bob stopped for a moment, looked at me, then said, "You stay with me and keep doing what you're doing." I complied. Ten minutes later, John came running back from the entrance of the cave and yelled, "Bob, we need you in the cave!" Bob took off running toward the cave. Half way there, he turned around, pointed at me, and said, "You! You're in charge!" Voila. That is how the wilderness facilitators (trained in wilderness rescue) took charge of organizing a very effective and efficient cave rescue. We did not intend to take charge. In fact, we had all agreed ahead of time we wanted to mostly observe at this event because we were all tired after a full summer of work. One lesson I learned at that event, is if I do not want to be in charge I should *not* take notes nor ensure accountability for decisions.

Accountability is vital. Answer the five questions, then record the answers in a system that remembers and reminds you.

Chapter 15—Effective Meetings

Do not merely look out for your own personal interests but also for the interests of others. – Philippians 2:4

Meetings are vital for existence. When two or more people get together to make one or more decisions, they are having a meeting, whether they realize it or not. We help each other, train each other, get to know each other, and make decisions together in meetings. Many people say they hate meetings. My experience is people despise bad meetings but enjoy skillful ones. To have the most skillful meeting possible people in the room need to:

1. Stay fully present and calm.
2. Have large positive emotional bank accounts with every person in the room.
3. Be quick to listen, slow to speak, and slow to anger.
4. Speak the truth in love.
5. Be up to date on forgiveness with every person in the room.
6. Be skilled at creative thinking.
7. Be skilled at fulfilling their roles within the group decision-making process.
8. Be skilled at crafting and following through with accountability.

I hear you thinking, "Yeah, that will never happen!" True. However, moving a few percentage points (say, from 30% to 35%) closer to that reality feels like a *huge* step toward unity. Just one highly skilled person in the room can move the group perhaps by as much as 10-20% closer (based on my experience) to the ideal. Imagine how wonderful it is to be in a meeting with many people proficient in the skills in this book. Do you want those kinds of meetings? It is possible!

Late 2006, I gave a power point presentation of the bare-bones principles in this book to the Discovery Ministries (DM) staff. We determined to live the principles in this book. Our progress showed clearest in the quality and satisfaction of our meetings. Many books have been written about meetings. The DM team focused on getting skilled at collaborative meetings. The remaining paragraphs of this section are the lessons the DM team learned about effective meetings. Most of these principles I have not read anywhere else. <u>My wife had me underline</u> the main point of each paragraph to make it easier for you to follow my mental meanderings.

The best way to focus on a decision is to <u>ask the right question.</u>[19] When the group understands this principle, they will get better at crafting questions that focus our efforts. For instance, "What do we want the entrance sign area to look like one year from now, and what accountability do we put in place to make that happen?" is a much better question than "How do we fix the entrance sign?"

Basically, a <u>meeting agenda is comprised of questions</u> we have yet to answer, and reports on previous solutions still in progress.

If you are sitting at your desk, walking down the hall, getting a drink, daydreaming at lunch, or otherwise minding your own business and you hear words like this, "Hey, can I ask you a quick question?" or "Hey, I would like to get your opinion on . . . ," <u>realize you are getting sucked into a loosy-goosy spontaneous meeting</u> that will easily waste *lots* of time.

The best question to ask <u>to quickly turn the corner towards</u> <u>an effective meeting</u> is, "What needs to happen, in this meeting (or conversation), so each of us goes away thinking it was an effective use of the next _____ minutes?" Notice, this forces us to develop our questions we want to answer, and it sets the time limit on the meeting. This principle revolutionized our spontaneous interactions at DM. We went from hours-long meandering conversations to effective 20-minute spontaneous meetings.

To <u>test the level of unity in a meeting</u>, stop the meeting, and have everyone write the answers to the following questions on a piece of paper. Then compare answers. In the ideal world, all the answers should be the same.

1. What question are we currently answering in the agenda?
2. Which stage of solution-finding are we on: defining the question, listing goals, creative thinking, deciding, or accountability?
3. If we are in the deciding phase, which decision-making process are we using?
4. What is the role of every person in the room at this point in the meeting?

The DM team used this test many times as we learned to have effective meetings. In the early days of our training, a perpetual question on our meeting agenda was, "What do we need to do better to make our meetings more effective?"

Each meeting needs a facilitator who prepares and runs the meeting. Let's just say we are going to have a two-hour meeting with ten people. If one person spends two hours to think through and prepare for it, we can finish in one meeting. If ten people just show up and start meeting without any prep time, it will probably take two or more meetings to make the same progress. Which is a better use of group time? With a facilitator, the group uses 22 people-hours (2 hours x 10 people + 2 hours of facilitator prep time). Without a facilitator, the group uses 40 people-hours (2 hours x 10 people x 2 meetings) for the same solutions. A low-skill facilitator saves people-hours. A highly skilled facilitator saves a *lot* of people-hours.

The facilitator changes roles depending on the current decision-making process. During collaboration, the meeting facilitator fills the role of neutral facilitator. If we are using a process where the leader decides, it is often best to have the facilitator step into a meeting-participant role, so the leader can walk the group through the solution for that question. After that solution, the leader turns the meeting back over to the facilitator.

We trained in meeting facilitation. The DM staff were experiential education facilitators. Some of those skills

143

transferred to meeting facilitation—reading the group's attention level, keeping people focused, listening for "Aha!" moments, etc. We also had to learn some new skills—the rest of the tidbits in this section. We designed the following to train ourselves. The people who wanted to learn meeting facilitation took turns facilitating. At the end of every meeting, every participant filled out an evaluation of the meeting, including the effectiveness of the facilitation. We also read as much as we cared to read about meeting facilitation, then tried new approaches on ourselves. We figured if we could facilitate meetings full of trained facilitators who are critiquing our every move, we could facilitate any meeting. It was great training.

The bane of a facilitator's existence are <u>the five-minute items</u>. Let's call them FMIs. No matter how hard you try to find out ahead of time what people want to talk about in the meeting, at least one person will show up with FMIs. Often, people remember in the middle of the meeting that they have FMIs. After much experimentation, here is how we handled FMIs. At the first of the meeting, the facilitator asked people to hold up their fingers showing the number of FMIs they had. Then, the facilitator quickly counted fingers, did the math, and knew how much time the group wanted to spend on FMIs. Everyone submitted to the facilitator's decision about how many FMIs to allow because they all

144

knew if they wanted to ensure a place on the agenda, they needed to let the facilitator know about the item a day or two before the meeting.

We need to use collaboration as our decision-making process much of the time because that is the only one that makes deposits in everyone's emotional bank accounts during the process. All other processes make withdrawals from many, if not all, of the members who have no say in the final decision.

We frequently use the five-finger assessment to show where everyone is on a collaborative decision. (One of my proof-readers said her group calls this "fist-to-five." Catchy!) Everyone must show one to five fingers when the facilitator calls for it. You can define the fingers any way you want. For instance:

1. One Finger: I am adamantly against this. If this is the solution, I will have to seriously consider whether I can remain a part of this group.

2. Two Fingers: I have serious reservations that prevent me from going along with this decision.

3. Three Fingers: I do not have a preference. I can support this decision as if it is my own.

4. Four Fingers: I think this is a good decision. I can easily support this decision as if it is my own.

5. Five Fingers: I think this is a great decision. I am excited to support it as if it is my own.

If the decision is not vital, if everyone shows three or more fingers, we go with it. The more vital the decision, the more hands need to show four or five fingers.

As a rule, introverts are the deep and thorough thinkers in a group. You want to take as much advantage of that gifting as possible. Here are a couple of tips to get the full benefit from introverts. Introverts think best when they are alone. Sometimes it is helpful to have the extroverts do a group dialog while the introverts each go to a quiet room to think and write. Then, bring them all back together to share ideas and continue the group dialog. Another tip—give introverts access to the agenda days before the meeting so they can stew on ideas for a while.

You can apply that introvert principle to all sorts of giftings. For instance, let creative and artistic people color during meetings, give fidgety people quiet squeeze toys, let engineers use tinker toys in the corner. Experiment to figure out what works best for all the gifted people in your group.

In collaboration, when a few group members are having a dialog and many other group members are just watching, it is time to form a sub-group. If a group member thinks the current question does not merit the effort of collaboration, then even collaboration is a withdrawal from that member's emotional bank account. Thus, it is vital for everyone in the group to voice when he/she thinks it is time to assign a sub-group. It is the facilitator's call when to form a sub-group. Here is the best way we found to form sub-groups. "Are you willing to abide by the sub-groups' decision as if it were your own?" If not, you are on the sub-group. Think about it in terms of people-hours. If three people have a dialog for 30 minutes while seven other people watch, the group just spent five people-hours on that dialog (.5 hours x 10 people). If those same three people have that dialog in a sub-group for 30 minutes, then give a five-minute report to the whole group, the group spent a little over two people-hours on that dialog (.5 hours x 3 people + 5 minutes x 10 people). Sub-groups save *lots* of group time and help maintain healthy emotional bank accounts.

When you form a sub-group, the date for their solution is put on the agenda and one person is assigned as the facilitator for the sub-group. It is that person's responsibility to run the sub-group meeting(s), liaison with the main group facilitator about how much time the sub-group report will take, and which kind of report they will present. A word on the type of sub-group reports, in our early experiments, we learned the hard way that sub-group reports easily, quickly, and naturally turn back into entire group discussions that start back at the beginning of the question. It is

147

disheartening, or worse, for sub-group members to watch all their work thrown aside. The group needs to develop discipline to accept the sub-group work as if it was the work of the entire group. To aid in this process, we developed codes that appeared on the agenda beside a sub-group's report. This prepared every group member to respond correctly to the sub-group. Of course, you can make up your own codes. We used:

1. FYI—This is a progress report. No discussion please.
2. ST—Skills training. Please adopt the role of student.
3. NR—We need resources, your input, or something else. Please limit the discussion to providing these resources.
4. OK—We are presenting the solution and accountability. The only discussion is if you see major red-flags we missed.
5. D—We need discussion with the entire group on a facet of the solution.

It takes practice for group members to effectively use sub-groups.

One person needs to take notes during the entire meeting, so we maintain a searchable record of our solutions. We also experimented with projecting the notes on a large screen as they were typed. The reason we started projecting was to ensure everyone felt heard—if you see your words on the screen, you know you were heard. In doing so, we stumbled onto a bigger benefit. When we projected the notes, the conversations got more thoughtful and thorough. A con—they also got slower; so, <u>the more vital and complicated the dialog, the more likely we were to project the notes</u>. If we needed to have quick discussions, we did not project the notes. See Appendix C for an example of a running agenda/notes.

<u>People will become effective contributors when they are convinced meetings are a worthwhile investment</u>. My experience is it takes five to ten effective meetings before people believe the meetings are valuable. The facilitator must bear all the hard work for those first meetings. Please stand firm in such a time as this. It is vital that the first ten meetings are effective! <u>Every group needs at least one person who can champion unity in meetings.</u>

When a collaborative group has <u>skilled weekly meetings</u>, they will quickly notice a negative impact on group unity when they miss one of those meetings.

There it is, my attempt to add to the existing meeting literature. I'm rooting for you. We're all in this together.

Chapter 16—Unity

How good and pleasant it is when God's people live together in unity!
– Psalm 133:1 NIV[30]

There it is—the training pyramid. Each skill lays an important foundation for the skills above it. Once your group has the skillsets in place to function with unity, it is challenging to maintain that high level of function. Unity ebbs and flows: someone gets sick; another person moves; a new person joins the group; life happens. How do you stay in unity? Besides practicing and using the skills in this book, the DM team developed four processes to maintain unity.

First, we trained every new person. If this book existed, it would have been part of the on-boarding reading list. Since it did not exist, each person got to sit through the two-hour seminar about the material in this book.

Next, every new person took all the assessments our staff used. We kept a confidential book in the office that showed staff's Myers Briggs Type,[12] Thomas-Kilmann Conflict Style,[5] Love Language,[13] and Forgiveness Language.[23] (A word of caution—we did make it permissible, and tried to make it safe, for people not to have one, or more, of their assessment results in the book. There are ethics involved here.) Only staff had access to the book. If "Bob" was having a challenging disagreement with "Linda", either of them could reference the book to refresh how best to interact with the other. There needs to be a lot of trust in the group to maintain a resource like this. Of course, you can design your own book using the assessments your group finds helpful.

Third, we used a quick survey twice per year. We got a forming-storming-norming-performing[2] survey from a book and tweaked it for our needs. (Here is one on the web, http://www.nwlink.com/~donclark/leader/teamsuv.html.)

The survey had about 30 questions. Each question allowed for an answer from one to four. Here are a couple of the questions we used:

1. Our collaborative dialogs take too long (1 = almost always, 4 = almost never).
2. Our collaborative dialogs don't last long enough (1 = almost always, 4 = almost never).

Our survey took each person about five to ten minutes to complete. I would gather the surveys, figure the average numbers for each answer, then put those averages on a spreadsheet, so we could see the trends for the overall survey and each answer. Our goal was to have 3.5 or higher on all questions. In the early days, the whole team looked at, and discussed, the survey results. Those dialogs took hours and were not very helpful; so, the team decided the co-directors should be a sub-group to evaluate the survey results, pick one area to work on for the next six months, then give a five-minute report to the team about the plan to raise our score. We also celebrated the areas that were continually strong. By the way, many of our solutions involved figuring out how to better match people's passions and giftings with the responsibilities of the survey area we wanted to improve.

Finally, it is appropriate to end this section, and this chapter, with our most important unity tool. Pray without ceasing. Pray the moment you feel any anxiety in the dialog.

Pray, it is more than a process. It is an individual and community lifestyle. It needs to be normal to include Jesus in every dialog. Pray—the challenges from Part I are hard. Pray—the solutions in Part II are hard. Pray—unity is dependent on Jesus. Pray—unity is incredibly challenging; so, give grace to yourself and those around you.

Part III—Adrenaline Sport Training

But I discipline my body and make it my slave, so that, after I have preached to others, I myself will not be disqualified.
– 1 Corinthians 9:27

I know I just wrote, "Pray—unity is dependent on Jesus." Yes, Jesus has to do His thing, *and* we have responsibility to learn, and conform to, His principles. Unity skills are an adrenaline sport. I came to that conclusion when I took interpersonal conflict resolution training as a person who had been a trainer in adrenaline sports for 15 years. I saw people physiologically respond in conflict resolution exercises the same way they responded when they got stuck in a cave. That is when it dawned on me, interpersonal skills, like the rules of any adrenaline sport, are easy to learn. The challenge is getting yourself to respond the way you know you should respond, rather than the way you naturally want to respond.

Reading a book about adrenaline skills is like reading a book on how to play basketball. No one expects an inexperienced basketball player to read a book about basketball, then immediately be able to play at the collegiate level. It takes years of practice to get good enough to do the skills under duress. Unity skills are the same way.

Many adrenaline sports rate the level of challenge. For instance, rivers are rated from Class I to Class VI. The way white-water paddlers think of the rating system is:

1. Class I—No skill required although you need to understand the basics and have respect for all moving water to prevent minor injuries and the loss of some of the stupid stuff you take on the river.

2. Class II—Basic paddling skills required to stay upright and prevent minor injuries.

3. Class III—Advanced paddling skills required to stay upright and prevent injuries.

4. Class IV—If you make a mistake you *will* swim, might lose some cool gear, and have a decent chance of getting injured.

5. Class V—If you make a mistake you will take a long swim, get injured, and probably lose significant amounts of your cool gear.

6. Class VI—If you make a mistake you will probably die and no longer care about your cool gear.

This rating system helps people figure out whether their skill level matches the water before they get on the water and find out the hard way. It also helps people realize when they need to get assistance to compensate for their lack of skill:

go with a group that is skilled at that level; hire a raft guide to take you through that wild water; take a class to get skill; etc.

Wouldn't it be great if we had a rating system for meetings between people, so you could know ahead of time whether your skill level matches the meeting or whether you need to make a plan to compensate for your lack of skill? Maybe the ratings would look something like this:

1. Class I—Close friends who will put up with almost anything as long as you stay within basic bounds of love and respect.

2. Class II—Basic interpersonal skills needed in order to stay together; i.e. stay married, keep your job.

3. Class III—Solid interpersonal skills needed to personally thrive: i.e. have a healthy marriage, advance in your job, step into leadership at church.

4. Class IV—Advanced interpersonal skills needed to maintain the health of the groups in which you exist; i.e. parenting, management, staff position at church or denominational headquarters.

5. Class V—Advanced interpersonal skills, with few mistakes, needed or people will get hurt. i.e. attempting to "turn around" a caustic team, C-level leadership, police answering a domestic disturbance call, family/marriage counseling, church and business dispute mediation.

6. Class VI—Significantly advanced interpersonal skills needed to prevent conflicts, wars, and collapses; i.e. national and global leadership positions in church, business, and government.

I suspect you now realize from looking at the above rating system, that you are in many class III and IV situations, yet you only have class I or II skill level. God forbid you are in Class V or VI situations with lack of skill.

That universal interpersonal conflict rating system does not yet exist. Until then, the point I am trying to make—you either need to train to bring unity to your groups, or get assistance from skilled facilitators, much like vacationers hire raft guides to have fun on whitewater.

Let's dive into the basics of training for adrenaline skills. I first learned these principles in Goddard and Neumann's Perfomance Rock Climbing.[7] Since then I have run across the principles in many venues, books, and articles. Here is my summary. There are five basic principles: develop good habits in easy circumstances; add challenge to develop more skill; reduce challenge to solidify basics; end each practice session with a success; and have grit for the duration.

Chapter 17—Develop Good Habits in Easy Circumstances

The brain works a specific way for skill development. When you first learn a skill, your brain must think through each step, which means you are slow performing the skill. When you repeat a skill, the brain creates shortcuts for those instructions, which means you can do it faster. It takes more repetitions to erase a shortcut and create a new one than it does to create a shortcut the first time. Under duress, your body does the shortcuts you have trained in your brain. Which means you need to be under zero duress to build the best foundational shortcuts.

Growing up, my family frequently went canoeing. My dad taught me paddling skills that were adequate for the easy rivers we paddled. However, the first time I went white-water canoeing, I found out how sloppy, and ineffective, my paddling form was. One paddling instructor told me if I had trained my forward stroke by throwing 2,000 sloppy forward strokes, I would have to do 4,000 good-form forward strokes before I would be able to throw a good forward stroke in big water. The most challenging element of training for me is the best place to develop whitewater strokes is on a lake (zero duress). Boring. I worked for years to overcome the sloppy strokes I learned growing up. *Many* of those hours were on non-moving water. Also, since I led week-long trips on Class I rivers most of the year, and only paddled Class III-IV eight to ten days per year, I quickly realized every stroke I threw in Class I water had to be good-form because every stroke in Class I built and reinforced the brain shortcuts my body would use in more challenging water. So much for relaxing and doing sloppy strokes on easy water.

When I started training in listening and speaking the truth in love, I scheduled quiet moments with willing practice partners to work on basics. I also quickly realized daily easy interactions developed the brain shortcuts I would use during disagreements and conflicts. Since I developed bad listening and speaking habits growing up, I had to get disciplined to learn good habits and use them in every interaction every day if I hoped to use them under duress. If I used sarcasm for fun during easy conversations, I would use sarcasm for attack during disagreements. If I interrupted in easy conversations, I would interrupt during disagreements. I think you get the point.

I realized I had to go back to the basics. I put the Equipping Ministries International Listening Sheet (See Appendix A) all over my house and office. I carried it with me. For months I used that formula in every conversation. My wife, family, and co-laborers at DM were very patient.

I also practiced staying calm by slowly breathing in through my nose and out through my mouth, and meditating on scripture, at least 15 minutes every morning, and as many times through the day as I remembered.

I did more training than this, I am just giving you some idea of how I went back to the basics and created righteous shortcuts. I practiced them for months and years to erase the natural, unhealthy, shortcuts I had developed in life.

Chapter 18—Add Challenge to Develop More Skill

Once brain shortcuts are developed in easy environments, you can start solidifying them in harder environments. The sad truth is when you get in an environment that is at the edge of your skill level, you revert to the practice you have done the most, which, for most of us, is slop. The solution is to keep pushing the edge of your skill level farther and farther out. You do that by pushing to the edge in environments that are as risk free as possible.

For years I looked like a limp doll in a wash machine when I tried to side surf in a canoe.

Side surf is dropping into a hole sideways. Water pouring into the hole from upstream tries to flip you. Water curling back into the hole from downstream tries to flip you. And you attempt to stay between them calm, upright, and able to move back and forth or spin as you desire.

Every time I tried, I freaked out and instantly flipped over. One sunny and warm day, Ronnie Beller, who knew how to side surf, and I happened on a challenging side-surf hole that was surrounded by gentle water and had quick access to dump the water out of the boat. I saw that spot and said, "Ronnie, I have tried for years to side surf. I never had an instructor, warm weather, and a good learning spot all happen at the same time. Do you mind if we stay here until I can side surf?" He agreed. We stayed in that spot for an hour or two. We didn't leave until I was comfortable side surfing in that very challenging hole (the hole was challenging, but the conditions surrounding it were not). From that day forward, I have been comfortable in side-surfs, even when a wild river unexpectedly sucks me into a gnarly one.

Here is the first way I applied this principle to listening training. I realized in the monthly business meeting at our church I spoke to almost every issue and usually sat in meetings thinking of what I would say next. I decided to not say anything in a meeting until I could calmly sit there having no preference. It was hard! After all, how could the church function without my thoughts? To get past that arrogant attitude deep in my psyche, I asked myself, "If I got hit by a car and died, would this church keep functioning?" Obviously, the answer was, "Yes." I reasoned with myself, I can sit in meetings with a smile on my face and not say anything, and the church will function. It took six months, six one-hour meetings, before I was able to sit in a meeting, breathe well, and meditate on scripture through the entire meeting. During those six months I re-learned the six points, from my trip journal, that I recorded in Chapter 9.

After I was able to sit calmly without needing to say anything, I began actively listening. If I heard a person say something that no one in the meeting acknowledged, I would raise my hand, get called on, look at the person, and use the Equipping Ministry International listening formula to prove to the person that he/she was heard. I was amazed how much positive difference staying calm and helping people feel heard made in a meeting. The whole meeting was more calm, focused, and effective. It was not my intent to transform the meetings. My intent was to practice staying calm, having no preference about the topic being discussed, and listening. It is miraculous that practicing scripture dramatically affects people around us.

To develop more skill, you must increase the challenge level of the practice. Basic ways to increase challenge are wean off cheat sheets, increase speed, increase complexity of surroundings, increase intensity of emotions, do more skills in succession, etc. For instance, if you want to get skilled at meditating, you might do the following progression:

1. Breathe well while you meditate.
2. Aim at what you want to hit—memorize scripture.
3. To increase challenge:
   a. Memorize a longer chunk of scripture— paragraph(s), chapter(s), book(s).
   b. Increase amount of time meditating.
   c. Increase challenge of environment:

i. Start in a quiet place with eyes closed. Once you can keep breathing well and have only scripture in your mind, then

ii. Open your eyes and look around. Once you can keep breathing well and have only scripture in your mind, then

iii. Go for a walk on a trail. Once you can keep breathing well and have only scripture in your mind, then

iv. Go for a walk in a crowded store. Once you can keep breathing well and have only scripture in your mind, then

v. Drive a car or bike. Once you can keep breathing well and have only scripture in your mind, then

vi. Go to a contentious meeting where you are not a participant. Once you can keep breathing well and have only scripture in your mind, then

vii. Go to a contentious meeting, where you are a participant, with the intent of staying calm and not speaking unless spoken to directly.

Chapter 19—Reduce Challenge to Solidify Skill

Yes, to increase skill, you increase challenge. However, to polish skill, you need to step back a level or two in challenge.

Remember the side-surf skill Ronnie Beller helped me develop? That day was not the last time I practiced that skill. I practice it *every* time I am on whitewater. I drop in the hardest side surfs I can find and try to stay upright—that expands the boundaries of my skill level. I also seek side surfs that are a level or two below my skill level—let's call these "gentle side surfs." When I am in a gentle side surf, I work on staying as calm as possible, breathing well, keeping my body in perfect position, keeping the boat at the perfect angle, and I use my paddle as little as possible. Hard side surfs become easier the more times I do this hard-easy-hard side-surf cycle. As a Class III paddler, I only thought Class I, and some Class II, side surfs were gentle. As a Class IV paddler, Class II, and some Class III, side surfs are gentle. My point is, drop back a level or two of challenge to work on good form. Dare to attempt a level higher to push the edge of your adrenaline response.

How does this apply in unity skills training? If I want to keep my skills honed, several times a week I sit down at family meals and focus on staying calm, actively listening, and speaking the truth in love. Other venues I use for practice are grocery stores, networking events, church gatherings, etc. A heated meeting is not the time to hone skills, it is the time to test skills.

Chapter 20—End Each Practice Session with a Success

I learned this in Rock Climbing, although I have noticed it applies in almost any training situation. Sometimes we would go out for a day and work all day on a climb just beyond our capability. It could get frustrating working hard to extend the boundaries of skill. The last climb of the day, we would do a climb at least one level below our ability, and we would do it with the best breath control, adrenaline control, and body form possible. Yes, this is like the principle of dropping back a level to hone skill. The difference is, this is an intentional attempt for my mind and body to end on a positive note.

How does this apply to unity skills training? If I am in an intense meeting and I make some unity mistakes, I find someone before walking out of the room and have a skillful dialog. If the meeting is done and all the people are gone before I realize I need to do this, I find a friend or family member ASAP and have a skillful dialog. This is different than debriefing from the meeting. It is just reminding my mind, body, and spirit that I do have skill.

When I catch myself in a mental or emotional slump at the end of a day of rock climbing or office meetings, often I realize the cause of the slump is that I neglected to end on a good note. Perhaps the point of this principle is to give myself a shot of hope and grace before walking away from a grueling practice session.

Chapter 21—Have Grit for the Duration

According to Jeff Wise, an investigative reporter who wrote a good book on fear and adrenaline,[6] Russian gymnastics coaches did not consider a move ready for competition until it was successfully completed 10,000 times in practice. That is a *lot* of good-form practice. Unity skills are no different. They take a *lot* of practice if you want to live them well during challenging situations. My opinion is it takes the average person, practicing an average amount of time, about five years to get skilled enough to effectively facilitate an average meeting.

The good news is I have had people excitedly tell me stories of using the skills, especially listening and forgiveness, the day after they learned them and seeing dramatic improvement in relationships and situations. There is a reason I think of these skills as miraculous.

Jesus can make an exception to the five-year learning curve. In the twinkle of an eye He can give a person skill that would normally take decades to develop. I have seen it. I have personally experienced it. I have also dealt with an interesting range of emotions as that gift faded when I sunk back to regular skill levels. Maybe the level I settled at was higher than where I was before Jesus stepped in and did His thing, but compared to feeling like the Holy Spirit was wielding the skills through me, wielding them as usual felt like driving five miles per hour by myself instead of 80 miles per hour with the Holy Spirit driving. Life is interesting. I just don't want you setting down this book thinking you are an expert after the first read. As a rule, you perform how you practice.

Apply these five principles of adrenaline sport training to the unity skills in this book, and you will find yourself stopping, with increasing frequency, to give thanks to Jesus for what you see happening around you.

Part IV—End and Begin

And they kissed each other and wept
together, but David wept the more
— 1 Samuel 20:41b

Unity is wonderful. Losing unity is like a close family member dying. Unfortunately, it is impossible to keep a group in unity for a lifetime because of minor and major upheavals: babies are born, school starts, children move out, co-workers change jobs, pastors leave, disasters strike, etc. Accepting this reality helps us get back to unity as quickly as possible after every challenging event. There are two main steps for getting back to unity: end and begin.

I should have seen it coming. After all, it happened at the end of every summer when the interns returned to college, and we all experienced the sadness of missing them. Why wouldn't it happen when I announce I'm leaving?

In the Fall of 2011, Colette and I announced our last day at DM would be January 31, 2012. We had planned for almost all facets of the transition, and things went according to plan, except for one surprise. In the middle of the excitement of getting ready to launch our new adventure in life, Colette, all our children, and I started struggling with sadness and depression. Colette and I prayed about it, then realized that, even though we were still in both groups, we were grieving the loss of all the wonderful relationships and ministry at DM and our church.

Ending requires grieving. A study on grief is beyond the scope of this book. Suffice it to say, there are three to seven stages of grief, depending on which research you read. Researchers agree grieving is different for different people and different events: the stages last for different amounts of time, go in different order, and can randomly repeat. Henry Cloud[31] explains that cathexis is investing mental and emotional resources into relationships and other goals. To have resources for the next goals, you must remove resources from previous goals—a process called decathect. Grieving is the way to decathect. A wise group knows how to say good-bye and grieve when a member departs.

Colette and I sat down with all the children and taught them about grieving. We acknowledged we each were suffering major loss as we risked something wonderfully new. We agreed to give each other freedom and space to grieve over the next year or so, until each of us felt settled in our new normal (a term I first heard in disaster response work). I think it took about three years for all the members of my family to finish grieving.

We also shared about grieving with our co-workers, church members, and extended family. Many of them indicated that having common understanding and language to talk about grief, helped ease some of the transition challenge. We gained first-hand knowledge of the reasons Bruce Tuckman modified his model to include a fifth stage: forming, storming, norming, performing, *and mourning*[2]. It is easier to move forward if you give yourself and others permission to grieve.

Groups need to end well.

They also need to immediately begin well. Every time a member of the group leaves or a new member joins, the group must go through the foundational stages of unity—forming, storming, and norming. A skilled group:

1. Quickly acquaints the new member(s) with the written and unwritten systems.

2. Reminds everyone of the reality of the need to practice every skill from Parts II and III of this book.

3. Plans to have a few meetings in the first few months to tweak group norms.

DM made great strides in effective on-boarding. We had to, because, every year, we doubled or tripled our staff size at the end of May and began intense ministry together by June first. During staff training week, in addition to teaching the basic tangible skills of running a camp, we:

1. Gave training in and assessed each new member's Myers-Briggs Type,[32] conflict style,[5] and love

language.[13] Then, with their permission, added their assessments to the Team Personalities Book.

2.   Made the Team Personalities Book required reading.

3.   Gave new members a two-hour seminar covering the basic principles of moving from muddling along to unity.

4.   Gave new members an intern manual and told them, "This manual is out of date. One of your assignments this summer is to correct every mistake you find in it. Given the reality that goals, plans, and roles constantly change, this manual will be out of date by the time you make corrections. That is why we always depend on the interns to keep the manual as current as possible."

5.   Assigned each intern a staff mentor. They met once per week during the summer. The staff mentor helped the interns bring any frustrations into the weekly staff meeting so we could tweak our systems.

Once we figured out this basic on-boarding system we consistently reached unity before the summer ended; some summers later than others.

As I mentioned, when the interns left at the end of the summer, it was a challenging time. Even though we were down to the same off-season staff as last year, it took us a few weeks to muddle through grieving while we reviewed the

174

off-season schedules and procedures to see how we needed to adjust them to fit all the ways we had changed over the summer.

We were willing to do the hard work every spring and every fall, because once we tasted unity, muddling along was an unappetizing option.

As with every concept in this book, you need to figure out ending and beginning in your own groups and contexts. What worked for DM might not work for you. I'm rooting for you. We are all together in this crazy world.

It is appropriate to close with the prayer Jesus prayed for us regarding this challenge of unity:

I do not ask on behalf of these alone, but for those also who believe in Me through their word; that they may all be one; even as You, Father, are in Me and I in You, that they also may be in Us, so that the world may believe that You sent Me. – John 17:20-21.

Amen.

Appendix A—Listen

NONVERBAL

Remember:
S - *Sensitive seating*
O - *Open posture*
L - *Leaning forward*
A - *Appropriate eye contact*
R - *Relaxing*

Also consider:
T - *Touching*
E - *Environment*
A - *Accommodating differences*

BASIC REFLECTIVE LISTENING FORMULA

Tentative opening +	Feeling +	About/because/when +	Thought
It sounds like...	you feel mad...	about...	paying higher taxes.
I hear saying that...	you feel sad...	because of...	what she said to you.
If I hear you correctly...	you feel glad...	when...	your sister succeed.
You seem to be saying...	you feel afraid...	about...	your father's ill health.
I think I hear you saying...	you feel confused...	because of...	all the different options.
I'm not sure I'm following...	you feel ashamed...	about...	wanting to leave home?
Am I hearing you say...	you feel lonely...	when...	you remember your wife?

FEELING WORDS:

MAD	SAD	GLAD	AFRAID	CONFUSED	ASHAMED	LONELY
A Little	A Little	A Little	A Little	A Little	A Little	A Little
Bothered	Down	At ease	Uneasy	Curious	Uncomfortable	Out of place
Ruffled	Blue	Secure	Apprehensive	Uncertain	Awkward	Left out
Irritated	Somber	Comfortable	Careful	Ambivalent	Clumsy	Unheeded
Displeased	Low	Relaxed	Cautious	Doubtful	Self-conscious	Lonesome
Annoyed	Glum	Contented	Hesitant	Unsettled	Disconcerted	Disconnected
Steamed	Lonely	Optimistic	Tense	Hesitant	Chagrined	Remote
Irked	Disappointed	Satisfied	Anxious	Perplexed	Abashed	Invisible
Perturbed	Worn-out	Refreshed	Nervous	Puzzled	Embarrassed	Unwelcome
Frustrated	Melancholy	Stimulated	Edgy	Muddled	Flustered	Cutoff
Angry	Downhearted	Pleased	Distressed	Distracted	Sorry	Excluded
Fed up	Unhappy	Warm	Scared	Flustered	Apologetic	Insignificant
Disgusted	Dissatisfied	Smug	Frightened	Jumbled	Ashamed	Ignored
Indignant	Gloomy	Happy	Repulsed	Unfocused	Regretful	Neglected
Ticked off	Mournful	Encouraged	Agitated	Fragmented	Remorseful	Separated
Bristling	Grieved	Tickled	Afraid	Dismayed	Guilty	Removed
Fuming	Depressed	Proud	Alarmed	Insecure	Disgusted	Detached
Explosive	Lousy	Cheerful	Shocked	Dazed	Belittled	Isolated
Enraged	Crushed	Thrilled	Overwhelmed	Bewildered	Humiliated	Unwanted
Irate	Defeated	Delighted	Frantic	Lost	Violated	Rejected
Incensed	Dejected	Joyful	Panic-stricken	Stunned	Dirty	Deserted
Burned	Empty	Elated	Horrified	Chaotic	Mortified	Outcast
Burned up	Wretched	Exhilarated	Petrified	Torn	Defiled	Abandoned
Outraged	Despairing	Overjoyed	Terrified	Baffled	Devastated	Desolate
Furious	Devastated	Ecstatic	Numb	Dumbfounded	Degraded	Forsaken
A Lot	A Lot	A Lot	A Lot	A Lot	A Lot	A Lot

Appendix B—Forgive

Innovative Alternatives, Inc.

18333 Egret Bay Blvd., STE 540 Houston, TX 77058

www.innovativealternatives.org   Off: 713-222-2525 or 832-864-6000

Steps to Forgiveness

When there is a great deal of unforgiveness and old hurts have been stacked one on top of the other, couples can feel stuck and may argue in circles for years, never really hearing each other. It is best to perform this process with a facilitator in these cases—a pastor, counselor or mediator. Once forgiveness is achieved, old wounds can heal and solutions to problems may be explored and agreed upon.

1. **Homework:** Each person in the relationship, make a list of behaviors for which you need to seek forgiveness. **Do not make a list of what the other person has done wrong.**

2. **Before you seek forgiveness:**
   a. **Pray** and ask God to reveal the hurt your behavior has caused and ask him to prepare your heart to seek forgiveness,
   b. **Be ready to turn away from the behavior.** 'Repentance' means to 'turn away from', so do not ask forgiveness if you intend to immediately commit the same act against this person. If you can't stop on your own, develop a plan and be ready to outline the plan and also to consider what the other person may need from you.
   c. **Humble yourself** and approach this process with a contrite heart. (Psalm 51:17)

3. **When asking for forgiveness:**

a. Name the offending behavior specifically. "I need to seek your forgiveness for the time(s) when I . . ."

b. Name the impact you believe this behavior has had on the other person. When I acted this way, I believe I _____ (hurt you, broke your trust in our relationship, embarrassed and humiliated you....) List as many consequences for your spouse, your relationship and others as the Lord brings to your mind. (This also caused our children great despair....)

c. Ask if you understand the full impact of your behavior on your loved one. "Have I touched on everything? Do I understand everything this did to you?"

d. Listen closely if any other consequences are disclosed, then be ready to repeat back what you heard. "So, in addition to what I thought this did to you, it also made you feel..., is that right?"

e. Ask them to forgive your specific behavior and list every way that they were affected. "Please forgive me for all the years of drinking uncontrollably. I am sorry that I hurt and embarrassed you in front of others; that I could not be trusted to drive with or to adequately parent our children. I'm sorry for all the times you felt disrespected and that I loved the alcohol more than my own family..."

f. If your hurtful behavior was something you need help or support to give up, present your plan for turning from the behavior. "I plan to form an accountability relationship with a spiritual mentor at church. I will call him/her when I am tempted to drink and ask him/her to pray with me. I will ask him/her to call to check on me if s/he doesn't hear from me once a week and if I can't be reached to call you. I intend to attend the Celebrate Recovery Group at __ church... I will check in with you when I go somewhere until I regain your trust...."

4. Before offering forgiveness:
   a. Check your heart and ask God to enable you to forgive—regardless of how you feel.
   b. Be ready to lay down your recounting, shaming and criticism of the past behavior. Believe they are turning away from it and pray for God to show you how to trust again. Do not offer forgiveness if you intend to continue beating the person up for this behavior—real forgiveness does not continue to seek punishment, but releases the person and the behavior to God.
   c. Speak your forgiveness as specifically as it was requested: "I forgive you completely for all the years your drinking was out of control and the times I was hurt, embarrassed and had my trust damaged because I felt so disrespected. I forgive you for the risks you took with our children and appearing to value the alcohol more than us."
5. Pray together. Ask the Holy Spirit to bless and seal this work by healing all old wounds and rebuilding the relationship that this sin had almost destroyed. Then pray together daily.

Revised 10/30/08

Appendix C—Meet

Sample Meeting Agenda

Facilitator for this meeting – David

Items we want to remember for every meeting

1. Types of Presentations – FYI, ST, NR, OK, D
2. The reasons we want to meet regularly
   a. To proactively maintain excellent relationships with each other
   b. Each of us learns to run meetings better in our other areas of influence
   c. This ministry stays at the cutting edge of faith and effectiveness
3. Start with prayer

Five-Minute Items (FMI) – Presenter and Item Type

1. Each FMI gets a line

Sub-Group (SG) Presentations – SG Facilitator, Presentation Due Date, Item Type

1. David – Due Date, ST, OK – Recommendation for publishing a magazine article
2. Colette – Due Date, OK – New brochure roll-out

Entire Group Decisions, Decision Process

1. Set date for five-year vision meeting, Leader Decides after Group Dialog
2. How should each intern be promoted, trained, or let go, Collaborate

Works Cited

[1] Wheelan, S. A. (2005). *Creating effective teams: A guide for members and leaders* (2nd ed.). Thousand Oaks, CA: Sage Publications, Inc.

[2] Tuckman forming storming norming performing model. (n.d.) Retreived July 22, 2017, from http://www.business balls.com/tuckmanformingstormingnormingperforming.htm

[3] Wilmot, W. W., & Hocker, J. L. (2001). *Interpersonal conflict* (6th ed.). Boston: McGraw-Hill.

[4] Senge, P. M. (2006). *The fifth discipline: The art & practice of the learning organization* (2nd ed.). Double Day: New York.

[5] Thomas, K. and Kilmann, R. (2007). *Thomas-Kilmann Conflict Mode Instrument Profile and Interpretive Report.* CPP. Available at https://www.cpp.com.

[6] Wise, Jeff (2009). *Extreme fear: The science of your mind in danger.* New York: Palgrave MacMillan.

[7] Goddard, D., & Neumann, U. (1993). *Performance rock climbing: Strength, endurance, tactics, technique.* Stackpole Books: Mechanicsburg, PA.

[8] Hughes, S. (2007). *My story: From welsh mining village to worldwide ministry* (Ext. ed.). Waverly Lane, Farnham, Surrey GU9 8EP CWR: Waverly Abbey House.

[9] Stone, D., Patton, B., & Heen, S. (1999). *Difficult conversations: How to discuss what matters most.* New York: Penguin Books.

[10] Peck, M. S. (1978). *The road less traveled: A new psychology of love, traditional values, and spiritual growth.* New York: Simon and Schuster.

[11] Cloud, H. (2010). *Necessary endings: The employees, businesses, and relationships that all of us have to give up in order to move forward.* New York: Harper-Collins Publishers.

[12] Myers-Briggs Type Indicator. Gainesville: Center for Applications of Psychological Type, Inc.

[13] Chapman, G. D. (2004). *The five love languages: how to express heartfelt commitment to your mate.* (3rd ed.). Chicago, IL: Northfield Publishing.

[14] Covey, S. R. (1989). *The 7 habits of highly effective people: Powerful lessons in personal change.* New York: Simon & Schuster.

[15] Marano, H. E. *Our brains's negative bias: Why our brains are more highly attuned to negative news. Psychology Today*. Retrieved December 4, 2017, from https://www.psychologytoday.com/articles/200306/our-brains-negative-bias

[16] Stone, D., Patton, B., & Heen, S. (1999). *Difficult conversations: How to discuss what matters most*. New York: Penguin Books.

[17] Wilmot, W. W., & Hocker, J. L. (2001). *Interpersonal conflict* (6th ed.). Boston: McGraw-Hill.

[18] Used with Permission from Equipping Ministries International, 110 Boffs Lane, Suite 301, Cincinnati, OH 45246. www.equippingministries.org. 800-364-4769.

[19] LaFasto, F. & Larson, C. (2001). *When teams work best: 6,000 team members and leaders tell what it takes to succeed*. Thousand Oaks: Sage Publications Inc.

[20] Paul Eckman's findings on micro expressions is some of the early research on this topic.

[21] Brauns, C. (2008). *Unpacking forgiveness: Biblical answers for complex questions and deep wounds*. Wheaton: Crossway Books.

[22] DeMoss, N. L. (2008). *Choosing forgiveness: Your journey to freedom*. (2nd ed.). Chicago, IL: Moody Publishers.

[23] Chapman, G., Thomas, J. (2006). *The five languages of apology: How to experience healing in all your relationships*. Chicago, IL: Northfield Publishing.

[24] Used with permission from Innovative Alternatives, Inc, 1335 Regent Park Drive, STE 240, Houston, TX 77058. www.innovativealternatives.org. 713-222-2525.

[25] Haren, Fredrik (2004). *The idea book*. Interesting Books: Stockholm, Sweden.

[26] Michalko, Michael (2006). *Thinkertoys: A handbook of creative-thinking techniques*. (2nd ed.). Berkeley: Ten Speed Press

[27] Coyne, K. P. & Coyne, S. T. (2011). *Brainsteering: The better approach to breakthrough ideas*. Harper Collins e-books: New York.

[28] Gordon T. Smith (2003) *The Voice of Jesus: Discernment, prayer and the witness of the spirit*. Grove, IL: Intervarsity Press.

[29] Mindtools.com. (2015). *The Vroom-Yetton-Jago Decision Model: Deciding How to Decide*. Retrieved May 7, 2018, from http://www.mindtools.com/pages/article/newTED_91.htm

[30] Holy Bible, New International Version®, NIV® Copyright © 1973, 1978, 1984, 2011 by Biblica, Inc.®

[31] Cloud, H. (2010). *Necessary endings: The employees, businesses, and relationships that all of us have to give up in order to move forward.* New York: Harper-Collins Publishers.

[32] Myers-Briggs Type Indicator. Gainesville: Center for Applications of Psychological Type, Inc.

Made in the USA
Middletown, DE
24 April 2019